The OSHA Training Answer Book

The Employer's Guide That Answers Every OSHA Training Question

2nd Edition

Mark M. Moran

SafetyCertified.com, Inc.
Jacksonville, Florida 32256
Phone: (904) 278-5155
Email: info@SafetyCertified.com
www.safetycertified.com

Second Edition   ISBN 0-9772214-2-3

Printed in the United States of America
2-10-2008 10 9 8 7 6 5 4 3 2

Library of Congress Control Number: 2002109890

Table of Contents

INTRODUCTION

The new OSHA Training Answer Book 2nd Edition includes all the latest changes in OSHA's Training standards. It includes the following new material:

- A sample Safety and Health Training plan
- Safety Training's Most Frequently Asked Questions (FAQ's)
- Safety Training Resources

This book will help you determine the workplace safety and health training OSHA requires. It does this in three ways:

- Offers guidelines to help you improve your existing training programs or to develop new ones;

- It summarizes, by topic, worker training required by OSHA; and

- Tells you where to find OSHA training requirements in General Industry Part 29 CFR 1910.

This book is designed to provide information on how to establish an effective training program and provides information on what employers need to know about OSHA training regulations. It is a reference book, designed to be consulted frequently.

This book will help employers decide when your workers need to be given the OSHA-mandated training for all of OSHA's training requirements including fire extinguishers, personal protective equipment (PPE), respirators, emergency procedures, Hazard Communication and forklift operations.

This book is divided into two parts:

- Part 1: How to develop a safety training program. It explains what OSHA's view on training is, how to design the training program, and what are OSHA's voluntary training guidelines.

- Part 2: What are the OSHA Training requirements? It explains all of them in General Industry 29 CFR 1910 training standards in every subpart by topic and summarizes the training required by OSHA.

How to use this book:

If you are an employer who wants to establish a training program or improve your existing one; or an employer who knows nothing about starting a training program, you should read Part 1. If you are an employer who wants to know what their OSHA training requirements are, you should read Part 2.

PART I:

HOW TO DEVELOP A SAFETY TRAINING PROGRAM

CHAPTER 1:

WHAT IS OSHA'S VIEW ON TRAINING?

OSHA requires employers to train workers in the safety and health aspects of their jobs. The requirements are not the same for all workplaces.

The most important step you can take toward developing a safe and healthful workplace is to think seriously about risk just as you would about any other business decision. You may not be able to eliminate risk in your work environment, but you can do a lot to minimize it. Training workers to do their jobs safely is only part of the picture.

You must be committed to minimizing workplace risks and you must have a sound safety and health program that puts your commitment into action. While there is no single safety and health program that works for all businesses, successful programs express the following beliefs:

- Management is responsible for preventing occupational Injuries;
- All injuries have preventable causes;
- On-the-job safety involves all workers;
- Preventing accidents is good business; and
- Workers must be trained to do their jobs safely.

What are OSHA's Training Requirements?

OSHA has general training requirements intended to make workers aware of the overall safety and health aspects of their jobs and specific training requirements that apply to workers who perform special jobs or tasks.

OSHA's safety and health requirements frequently use the words *certified, designated, authorized, competent person,* and *qualified person* to identify workers who must meet specific training requirements.

Certified indicates that a worker has successfully completed specialized training and that the training has been certified in writing by a professional organization. For example, OSHA's safety and health rules allow only trained audiologists, otolaryngologists, or technicians who have been certified by the Council of Accreditation in Occupational Hearing Conservation to perform audiometric tests.

Designated generally refers to a person who has received extensive training in a particular task and is assigned by the employer to perform the task.

Authorized refers to a person permitted by an employer to be in a regulated area; the term also refers to a person assigned by an employer to perform a specific task or to be in a specific location at a jobsite.

A *competent person* is someone who has broad knowledge of worksite safety and health issues, who is capable of identifying existing and predictable worksite hazards, and who has management approval to control the hazards. Only a competent person for example, can supervise erecting, moving, or dismantling scaffolds at a worksite.

A *qualified person* is someone who, through training and professional experience, has demonstrated the ability to resolve problems relating to a specific task or process. For example, an individual may be qualified to perform electrical circuit tests but not qualified to perform hydraulic pressure tests.

What Workplace Training Can Do to Help Your Workers

Worker training is an essential element of every employer's safety and health program. The time and money it takes to train workers is an investment that pays off in fewer workplace accidents and lower insurance premiums.

Training also helps inexperienced workers who tend to have higher injury and illness rates than experienced workers. However, training isn't likely to help if workers don't understand it, if they are unmotivated, or if managers and supervisors don't enforce safe work practices.

Effective training requires planning, dedicated instructors, and motivated students. It doesn't matter whether the topic is athletics, academics, or workplace safety; the steps for successful training are similar:

- Design the training program;
- Conduct the training; and
- Evaluate the training's effectiveness.

How to Design the Training Program

Can worksite problems be solved by training?

If workers are using a new, heavier nail gun experience more shoulder injuries than they did with an older model, for example, the injuries may be related to the way they hold the gun or to the gun's weight.

There may be a proper way to hold the gun, a problem that could be solved by training or the gun may simply be too heavy a problem that could be solved by using a lighter model. You may need to modify equipment or a work process to control a hazard and design a training program to educate workers about the changes.

Identify hazardous task - Evaluate the tasks to determine what workers must learn to do their jobs safely.

Develop learning activities - Learning activities enable workers to demonstrate that they've acquired the skills to do their jobs safely. The activities should simulate actual job tasks as closely as possible. You can make the activities group-oriented through lectures and role-playing, or you can develop self-paced activities for individuals.

Plan the training structure and format - Consider the number, frequency, and length of sessions. Determine the instructional techniques and who will do the training.

Make sure training sessions have clearly defined objectives and are relevant to workers' jobs. Give workers an overview of what they'll learn. Include hands-on and role-playing activities if possible. Reinforce learning by summarizing objectives and key concepts. Let workers participate in discussions.

How to Evaluate the Training's Effectiveness

Make sure the training accomplishes your objectives. Ask supervisors if workers are accomplishing their training goals, review injury and illness statistics for trends that training may have influenced, and consider the following:

- Did the training focus on critical elements of the job?

- Did the training cover gaps in workers' knowledge or skills?

- Were the training objectives presented clearly?

- Did the objectives state what performance levels you expected from the workers?

- Did learning activities simulate work tasks?

- Were learning activities appropriate for the knowledge and skills the jobs required?

- Were training materials organized and presented clearly?

- Were the workers motivated to learn?

- Were the workers encouraged to participate and to ask questions?

How to Identify Workers Who Do High-risk Jobs

Workers exposed to heat, noise, falls, chemicals, or mechanical hazards may need special training, particularly if their injury and illness rates are consistently higher than industry-wide rates from comparable jobs.

Remember that work related accidents may be caused by poor workplace design and work processes as well as inadequate training.

What are OSHA's Training Obligations?

As an employer, your OSHA training obligations are to observe all applicable occupational safety and health training standards (OSHA standards) promulgated by the Secretary of Labor. What employees they cover and who must comply with them is explained in this book.

Most OSHA citations to date have alleged violations of OSHA training standards. Understanding and observing them is, therefore, the most important employer responsibility. An explanation of what they cover and who must comply is included in the section on OSHA training standards.

There are more than 100 OSHA standards that require the employer to train employees in the safety and health aspects of their jobs. These requirements reflect OSHA's belief that training is an essential part of every employer's safety and health program for protecting workers from injuries and illnesses.

Many researchers conclude that those who are new on the job have a higher rate of accidents and injuries than more experienced workers. If ignorance of specific job hazards and of proper work practices is even partly to blame for these higher injury rates, then training will help to provide a solution.

As an example of the latest trends in OSHA training requirements, the Process Safety Management of Highly Hazardous Chemicals Standard 29 CFR 1910.119 contains several training requirements:

> The Process Safety Management Standard requires the employer to evaluate or verify that employees comprehend the training given to them. This means that the training to be given must have established goals and objectives regarding what is to be accomplished. Subsequent to the training, an evaluation would be conducted to verify that the employees understood the subjects presented or acquired the desired skill.

The length and complexity of OSHA standards make it difficult to find all the references to training requirements. So, to help employers, safety and health professionals, training directors, and others with a need to know, OSHA's training-related requirements have been excerpted and collected in this book.

It is a good idea for the employer to keep a record of all safety and health training. Records can provide evidence of the employer's good faith and compliance with OSHA standards. Documentation can also supply an answer to one of the first questions an OSHA Inspector will ask: "Was the injured employee trained to do that job?" Training in the proper performance of a job is time and money well spent. The employer should regard it as an investment rather than an expense. An effective program of safety and health training for workers can result in fewer injuries and illnesses, better morale, and lower insurance premiums, among other benefits.

What Employees should be Trained?

Safety and health training should cover the safety and health responsibilities of all personnel who work at the company. It is most effective when it is incorporated into other training about performance requirements and job practices. It should include all subjects and areas necessary to address the hazards in the workplace.

OSHA considers safety and health training vital to every workplace and it is an important component of a comprehensive program. Training helps employees develop the knowledge and skills they need to understand workplace hazards and how to handle them in order to prevent or minimize their own exposure.

Before training begins, be sure that the company policy clearly states the company's commitment to health and safety and to the training program. This commitment must include paid work time for training. The training should be in the language that the employee understands and at a level of understanding appropriate for the individuals being trained. Both management and employees should be involved in the development and delivery of the program.

Documentation of training must be maintained where training is required by a standard. OSHA requires that such documentation be available for review by compliance officers in the event of an inspection. Documentation of training assures that initial or periodic training is accomplished within established time frames.

New employees need to be trained not only to do the job, but also to recognize, understand and avoid potential hazards to themselves and others in the workplace. Contract workers also need training to recognize the hazards of the workplace. Experienced workers will need training if new equipment is installed or a process changes. Employees needing to wear personal protective equipment and persons working in high risk situations will need special training.

Training New Workers

The confusion and stress that accompany the first days of any job are the reasons that new employees are more than twice as likely to have an accident as experienced workers. Lack of experience, a strong desire to please, and hesitation to ask for help all cause one in eight new employees to be involved in some type of accident the first year on the job. The first month is the most critical.

These are also the formative days on the job. New employees are ready to learn and eager to succeed. They are also very receptive to both structured and informal training, if offered. As a supervisor, you are one of the first people new employees turn to. Your role is to shape their behavior and performance. Training that stresses safety can be the perfect opportunity for you to establish rapport with the worker.

What Training Should be Covered?

All employees' training should include an introduction to the company's training program. It is your job as the supervisor to answer any questions and make sure employees understand the training.

New employees need to know how attention to safety in their jobs relates to the overall function of the department and the company. Include the relevant safety precautions in the employee's job descriptions and give each new employee a copy as well as any safety publications. At every phase of training, discuss the company's commitment to safety.

Explain safety rules and emergency procedures. Point out the location of first-aid facilities. Explain how and when to use personal protective equipment and how to care for it. Make sure the employee understands the importance of the procedures. Encourage new employees to report unsafe conditions to you, as well as any accidents, even if there are no injuries or property damage.

Are All OSHA Training Requirements the Same?

OSHA's training requirements vary greatly from standard to standard. The OSHA standards that cover employee training vary from the specific to the general, with the vast majority of them falling into the latter category. For example, OSHA's Powered Industrial truck standard 29 CFR 1910.178 states:

> The employer shall ensure that each powered industrial truck operator is competent to operate a powered industrial truck safely, as demonstrated by the successful completion of the training and evaluation.

Similar requirements are scattered throughout the entire body of OSHA training standards.

OSHA training requirements are all different in the scope and complexity of the conditions addressed by the standards. The discussion below elaborates on the variable nature of the training rules with regard to factors such as content, frequency/duration, documentation/assurance, trainer qualifications, and methods used.

Content

A number of standards are quite explicit about what safe practices should be taught. Training rules for pulpwood logging are of this nature. For example OSHA's Logging

Standard 29 CFR 1910.266 states:

> "Chainsaw operators shall be instructed to start the saw at least 10 feet away from the fueling area."

Still other training standards acknowledge topics to be covered (e.g., recognition of hazardous conditions, risk factors and potential outcomes, needs for and means for hazard control) but do not go any further, thus leaving the specific content up to the employer.

Frequency/Duration

Standards covering exposures to toxic agents dictate that employees receive training before an initial job assignment and repeat training on some periodic basis. For example, OSHA's Hazardous Waste and Emergency Response Standard 29 CFR 1910.120 states that:

> Minimum durations for initial training offsite and supervised onsite instruction plus yearly refresher training.

At the other extreme, a number of other training standards make no reference either to the duration of required training or to the need for repeat or follow-up instruction.

Documentation

Some OSHA training standards require evidence of a formal training plan. For example OSHA's Noise Standard 29 CFR 1910.95 states:

> You must have an annual training program for workers exposed to noise at or above an eight-hour time-weighted average of 85 decibels. The program must be consistent with changes in personal protective equipment and work processes. Workers exposed to high noise levels must be fitted with hearing protectors and trained how to use and care for them and provide all training and education program materials to OSHA upon request.

The language in most other training standards is less specific about the needs for a formalized training program, records of employee participation, or achievement. A number of other training standards indicate that employees shall demonstrate proficiency following instruction but do not actually require certification.

Trainer Qualifications and Training Certification

Some OSHA training standards indicate teaching requirements for those slated to instruct employees or stipulate tasks to be undertaken by competent persons. Competent persons are defined as those having acquired necessary skills by virtue of attending training schools, holding academic degrees, or possessing specialty experience.

Related to this point, OSHA's Hazardous Waste Operations and Emergency Response standard 29 CFR 1910.120 states:

Trainers shall be qualified to instruct employees about the subject matter that is being presented in training. Such trainers shall have satisfactorily completed a training program for teaching the subjects they are expected to teach, or they shall have the academic credentials and instructional experience necessary for teaching the subjects. Instructors shall demonstrate competent instructional skills and knowledge of the applicable subject matter. *Training certification* - Employees and supervisors that have received and successfully completed the training and field experience shall be certified by their instructor or the head instructor and trained supervisor as having completed the necessary training. A written certificate shall be given to each person so certified. Any person who has not been so certified or who does not meet the requirements shall be prohibited from engaging in hazardous waste operations.

Some OSHA training standards do not dictate methods to be used in meeting the required training objectives. Several other training standards stipulate a portion of the training time to be a "hands-on" learning experience.

More generally, however, the "how to" of training is left to the discretion of the employer. For example, OSHA's Powered Platform Standard 29 CFR 1910.66 states:

> Pictorial methods can be used instead of written work procedures in the training activity.

What are OSHA's Voluntary Training Guidelines?

OSHA has developed training guidelines to assist employers in safety and health information and instruction to workers. The guidelines are voluntary and are meant to enhance or supplement other employer training activities. Tailoring their application to meet individual worksite needs or local working conditions is encouraged. The OSHA voluntary training guidelines follow a model whose elements reiterate general job training.

The model addresses the questions of who should be trained, on what topics, and for what purposes. It also helps employers determine how effective the program has been and enables them to identify employees who are in greatest need of education and training. The model is general enough to be used in any area of occupational safety and health training.

There are seven guidelines that are covered below. The guidelines are designed to help employers with the following:

- Determine whether a worksite problem can be solved by training;

- Determine what training, if any, is needed;

- Identify goals and objectives for the training;

- Design learning activities;

- Conduct training;

- Determine the effectiveness of the training; and

- Revise the training program based on feedback from employees, supervisors and others.

The development of the guidelines is part of OSHA's objective to encourage cooperative, voluntary safety and health activities among OSHA, the business community and workers. These voluntary programs include training and education, consultation, voluntary protection programs, and abatement assistance.

The guidelines provide employers with a model for designing, conducting, evaluating, and revising training programs. The training model can be used to develop training programs for a variety of occupational safety and health hazards identified at the workplace.

It can also assist employers in their efforts to meet the training requirements in current or future occupational safety and health standards. A training program designed in accordance with these guidelines can be used to supplement and enhance the employer's other education and training activities.

The guidelines should give employers significant flexibility in the selection of content and training program design. OSHA encourages a personalized approach to the informational and instructional programs at individual worksites, thereby enabling employers to provide the training that is most needed and applicable to local working conditions.

Employee training programs are always an important issue in cases that involve alleged violations of training requirements contained in OSHA standards. The adequacy of employee training may also become an issue in contested cases where the affirmative defense of unpreventable employee misconduct is raised.

Under case law well established by OSHA, an employer may successfully defend against an otherwise valid citation by demonstrating that all feasible steps were taken to avoid the occurrence of the hazard, and that actions of the employee involved in the violation were a departure from a uniformly and effectively enforced work rule of which the employee had either actual or constructive knowledge.

In either type of case, the adequacy of the training given to employees in connection with a specific hazard is a factual matter that can be decided only by considering all the facts and circumstances surrounding the alleged violation.

The model is designed to be one that even the owner of a business with very few employees can use without having to hire a professional trainer or purchase expensive training materials. Using this model, employers or supervisors can develop and administer safety and health training programs that address problems specific to their own business, fulfill the learning needs of their own employees, and strengthen the overall safety and health program of the workplace.

OSHA's Voluntary training provides the elements to develop a good training program. The employer should become familiar with the seven steps for program development and be able to use them to plan a good training program. Safety training should be a part of every employee's basic job training. This reinforces the belief that safety is an essential part of the job. By focusing on job training needs, you will identify safety training needs. You want your employees to learn what they need to know and will use in their job performance. Follow these steps for an effective training program:

Step #1 – How to Determine Training Needs

Training does not solve all problems. Sometimes the problem may be work procedures, equipment, or lack of employee motivation. Ask yourself, "Could the employee do the job if he wanted to?" If the answer is "yes" then training may be less effective (but can still be used). "Does the employee have the skills or knowledge to perform the job?"

If the answer is "no," then training will probably benefit the employee. Training may need to be done due to:

- Employee's lack of knowledge;
- Employee's lack of skills;
- New machinery or equipment;
- New procedures or job change; and
- Any aspects of behavior needing to be changed.

Some training may be required by federal, state, or local laws, such as OSHA, local fire departments, or other local regulatory agencies.

> All new employees need to participate in an overall safety training orientation class. Every employee must be trained to be aware of and understand the hazards in the workplace.

After you have determined that training will correct the problems and/or meet the legally mandated training, the next step is to identify the training needs.

Step #2- How to Identify Training Needs

If the problem is one that can be solved, in whole or in part, by training, then the next step is to determine what training is needed. For this, it is necessary to identify *what* the employee is expected to do and in what ways, if any, the employee's performance is deficient.

This information can be obtained by conducting a job analysis that pinpoints what an employee needs to know in order to perform a job. When designing a new training program, or preparing to instruct an employee in an unfamiliar procedure or system, a job analysis can be developed by examining engineering data on new equipment or the material safety data sheets on unfamiliar substances.

The content of the specific federal or state OSHA standards applicable to a business can also provide direction in developing training content. Another option is to conduct a job hazard analysis. This is a procedure for studying and recording each step of a job, identifying existing or potential hazards, and determining the best way to perform the job in order to reduce or eliminate the risks. Information obtained from a job hazard analysis can be used as the content for the training activity.

If an employee's learning needs can be met by revising an existing training program rather than developing a new one, or if the employee already has some knowledge of the process or system to be used, appropriate training content can be developed through such means as:

- Using company accident and injury records to identify how accidents occur and what can be done to prevent them from recurring;

- Requesting employees to provide, in writing and in their own words, descriptions of their jobs. These should include the tasks performed and the tools, materials and equipment used;

- Observing employees at the worksite as they perform tasks, asking about the work and recording their answers;

- Examining similar training programs offered by other companies in the same industry.

The employees themselves can provide valuable information on the training they need.

> Safety and health hazards can be identified through the employees' responses to such questions as whether anything about their jobs frightens them, if they have had any near miss incidents, if they feel they are taking risks, or if they believe that their jobs involve hazardous operations or substances.

A second method of identifying employee populations at high levels of risk is to examine the incidence of accidents and injuries, both within the company and within the industry.

If employees in certain occupational categories are experiencing higher accident and injury rates than other employees training may be one way to reduce that rate. In addition, thorough accident investigation not only can identify specific employees who could benefit from training but can also identify company-wide training needs.

Research has identified the following variables as being related to a disproportionate share of injuries and illnesses at the worksite on the part of employees:

- The age of the employee (younger employees have higher incidence rates);

- The length of time on the job (new employees have higher incidence rates);

- The size of the firm (in general terms, medium-size firms have higher incidence rates than smaller or larger firms);

- The type of work performed (incidence and severity rates vary significantly by SIC code); and

- The use of hazardous substances (by SIC code).

These variables should be considered when identifying employee groups for training in occupational safety and health.

Step #3 – How to Identify Training Goals and Objectives

Once the kind of training that is needed has been determined, it is equally important to determine what kind of training is not needed. Employees should be made aware of all the steps involved in a task or procedure, but training should focus on those steps on which improved performance is needed. This avoids unnecessary training and tailors the training to meet the needs of the employees.

Once the employees' training needs have been identified, employers can then prepare objectives for the training. Instructional objectives, if clearly stated, will tell employers what they want their employees to do, to do better or to stop doing.

Learning objectives do not necessarily have to be written, but in order for the training to be as successful as possible, clear and measurable objectives should be thought out before the training begins. For an objective to be effective, it should identify as precisely as possible what the individuals will do to demonstrate that they have learned, or that the objective has been reached. They should also describe the important conditions under which the individual will demonstrate competence and define what constitutes acceptable performance.

Using specific, action-oriented language, the instructional objectives should describe the preferred practice or skill and its observable behavior. For example, rather than using the statement: "The employee will understand how to use a respirator" as an instructional objective, it would be better to say: "The employee will be able to describe how a respirator works and when it should be used."

Objectives are most effective when worded in sufficient detail that other qualified persons can recognize when the desired behavior is exhibited.

Training Employees at Risk

Determining the content of training for employee populations at higher levels of risk is similar to determining what any employee needs to know, but more emphasis is placed on the requirements of the job and the possibility of injury. One useful tool for determining training content from job requirements is the job hazard analysis described earlier. This procedure examines each step of a job, identifies existing or potential hazards, and determines the best way to perform the job in order to reduce or eliminate the hazards. Its key elements are:

- Job description;
- Job location;
- Key steps (preferably in the order in which they are performed);
- Tools, machines, and materials used;
- Actual and potential safety and health hazards associated with these key job steps; and
- Safe and healthful practices, apparel and equipment required for each job step.

Material safety data sheets can also provide information for training employees in the safe use of materials. For example:

> The Material Safety Data Sheets, developed by chemical manufacturers and importers, are supplied with manufacturing or construction materials and describe the ingredients of a product, its hazards, protective equipment to be used, safe handling procedures, and emergency first aid responses. The information contained in these sheets can help employers identify employees in need of training (i.e., workers handling substances described in the sheets) and train employees in safe use of the substances.

Material safety data sheets are generally available from suppliers, manufacturers of the substance, and large employers who use the substance on a regular basis, or they can be developed by employers or trade associations. MSDSs are particularly useful for those employers who are developing training on chemical use as required by OSHA's Hazard Communication Standard.

Step #4 – How to Develop Learning Activities

Once employers have stated precisely what the objectives for the training program are, then learning activities can be identified and described. Learning activities enable employees to demonstrate that they have acquired the desired skills and knowledge. To ensure that employees transfer the skills or knowledge from the learning activity to the job, the learning situation should simulate the actual job as closely as possible.

Thus, employers may want to arrange the objectives and activities in a sequence that corresponds to the order in which the tasks are to be performed on the job, if a specific process is to be learned. For instance, if an employee must learn the beginning processes of using a machine, the sequence might be the following:

- To check that the power source is connected;
- To ensure that the safety devices are in place and are operative; and
- To know when and how to throw the switch; etc.

A few factors will help to determine the type of learning activity to be incorporated into the training. One aspect is the training resources available to the employer. Can a group training program that uses an outside trainer and film be organized, or should the employer personally train the employees on a one-to-one basis? Another factor is the kind of skills or knowledge to be learned. Is the learning oriented toward physical skills (such as the use of special tools) or toward mental processes and attitudes?

Such factors will influence the type of learning activity designed by employers. The training activity can be group-oriented, with lectures, role-play and demonstrations; or designed for the individual as with self-paced instruction.

The determination of methods and materials for the learning activity can be as varied as the employer's imagination and available resources will allow. For example:

> The employer may want to use charts, diagrams, manuals, slides, films, viewgraphs (overhead transparencies), videotapes, audiotapes, or simply blackboard and chalk, or any combination of these and other instructional aids. Whatever the method of instruction, the learning activities should be developed in such a way that the employees can clearly demonstrate that they have acquired the desired skills or knowledge.

Step #5 –How to Conduct the Training

With the completion of the steps outlined above, the employer is ready to begin conducting the training. To the extent possible, the training should be presented so that its organization and meaning are clear to the employees. To do so, employers or supervisors should:

- Provide overviews of the material to be learned;

- Relate, wherever possible the new information or skills to the employee's goals, interests, or experiences; and

- Reinforce what the employees learned by summarizing the program's objectives and the key points of information covered.

These steps will assist employers in presenting the training in a clear, unambiguous manner.

In addition to organizing the content, employers must also develop the structure and format of the training. The content developed for the program, the nature of the workplace or other training site, and the resources available for training will help employers determine for themselves the frequency of training activities, the length of the sessions, the instructional techniques and the individual(s) best qualified to present the information.

In order to be motivated to pay attention and to learn the material the employer or supervisor is presenting, employees must be convinced of the importance and relevance of the material. Some ways to develop motivation include:

- Explaining the goals and objectives of instruction;

- Relating the training to the interests, skills and experiences of the employees;

- Outlining the main points to be presented during the training session(s);and

- Pointing out the benefits of training (e.g., the employee will be better informed, more skilled and thus more valuable both on the job and in the labor market; or the employee will, if he or she applies the skills and knowledge learned, be able to work at reduced risk).

An effective training program allows employees to participate in the training process and to practice their skills or knowledge. This will help to ensure that they are learning the required knowledge or skills and permit correction if necessary. Employees can become involved in the training process by participating in discussions, asking questions, contributing their knowledge and expertise, learning through hands-on experiences, and through role-playing exercises.

Step #6 – How to Evaluate the Training Program

To make sure that the training program is accomplishing its goals, an evaluation of the training can be valuable. Training should have, as one of its critical components, a method of measuring the effectiveness of the training. A plan for evaluating the training session(s), either written or thought-out by the employer, should be developed when the course objectives and content are developed. It should not be delayed until the training has been completed. Evaluation will help employers or supervisors determine the amount of learning achieved and whether an employee's performance has improved on the job. Among the methods of evaluating training are:

- *Student opinion* - Questionnaires or informal discussions with employees can help employers determine the relevance and appropriateness of the training program

- *Supervisors' observations* - Supervisors are in good positions to observe an employee's performance both before and after the training and note improvements or changes; and

- *Workplace improvements* - The ultimate success of a training program may be changes throughout the workplace that result in reduced injury or accident rates.

However it is conducted, an evaluation of training can give employers the information necessary to decide whether the employees achieved the desired results, and whether the training session should be offered again in the future.

Step #7 – How to Improve the Training Program

If, after evaluation, it is clear that the training did not give the employees the level of knowledge and skill that was expected, then it may be necessary to revise the training program or provide periodic retraining. At this point, asking questions of employees and of those who conducted the training may be of some help. Among the questions that could be asked are:

- Were parts of the content already known and, therefore, unnecessary?

- What material was confusing or distracting?

- Was anything missing from the program?

- What did the employees learn, and what did they fail to learn?

It may be necessary to repeat steps in the training process, that is, to return to the first steps and retrace one's way through the training process. As the program is evaluated, the employer should ask:

- If a job analysis was conducted, was it accurate?

- Was any critical feature of the job overlooked?

- Were the important gaps in knowledge and skill included?

- Was material already known by the employees intentionally omitted?

- Were the instructional objectives presented clearly?

- Did the learning activity simulate the actual job?

- Was the learning activity appropriate for the kinds of knowledge and skills required on the job?

- When the training was presented, was the organization of the material and its meaning clear?

- Were the employees allowed to participate actively in the training process?

- Was the employer's evaluation of the program thorough?

A critical examination of the steps in the training process will help employers to determine where course revision is necessary.

CHAPTER 2:

WHICH EMPLOYEES REQUIRE SAFETY TRAINING?

Can employees explain every existing and potential hazard to which they are exposed? Do they know how to protect themselves and their coworkers from these hazards? Can they explain precisely what they must do in the event of a fire or other emergency?

Most employers do not have the answers to the above questions. Training can help employees develop the knowledge and skills they need to understand workplace hazards. OSHA considers safety and health training vital to every workplace.

Before training begins, be sure that your company policy clearly states the company's commitment to health and safety and to the training program. This commitment must include paid work time for training and training in the language that the worker understands. Involve both management and employees in developing and delivering the programs.

New employees require training not only to do the job, but are required by the law, to recognize, understand, and avoid potential hazards to themselves and others in their immediate work area and elsewhere in the workplace. Contract workers also need training to recognize your workplace's hazards or potential hazards.

Experienced workers will need training if new equipment is installed or process changes. Employees needing to wear personal protective equipment and persons working in high risk situations will need special training.

A training program should be available to each new employee. This is true for all employment levels of management, supervisory, or worker. New employees are usually open to ideas and information about the way business is done. From the first day, new employees begin to formulate opinions about the company, managers, supervisors, and fellow workers.

Training instruction is a key issue in the orientation of new employees. Managers must be aware of the company's policies and mission statements concerning worker safety and health prior to making decisions that affect work processes. Similarly, new workers must have an early understanding of the organization's safety and health policies that safeguard them in the performance of their assigned tasks.

The list of training topics chosen for an employee training program largely depends on the audience. Subjects will vary if an organization provides separate classes for managers and workers. All of the topics below should be provided training prior to actual work exposure. They include the following:

- Hazard communication
- Personal protective equipment
- Emergency response procedures, (such as fire and spill)
- Accident reporting procedures
- Recording injuries and illnesses
- Accident investigation (supervision)
- Lockout/tagout procedures
- Machine guarding
- Electrical safety awareness
- Ladder use and storage

- Confined space entry
- First aid and CPR
- Hand tool safety
- Ergonomic principles
- Eye wash and shower locations
- Fire prevention and protection and
- Access to exposure and medical records

Types of Employee Training

Employees need to be trained not only to do the job, but also to recognize, understand, and avoid potential hazards to themselves and others in their immediate work area and elsewhere in the workplace. Contract workers also need training to recognize your workplace's hazards or potential hazards. Experienced workers will need training if new equipment is installed or process changes. Employees needing to wear personal protective equipment and persons working in high risk situations will need special training. A list of specialized employee training follows:

Periodic Safety and Health Training

Some worksites need complex work practices to control hazards. Some worksites experience fairly frequent occupational injuries and illnesses. At such sites, it is especially important that employees receive periodic safety and health training to refresh their memories and to teach new methods of control. New training also may be necessary when OSHA or industry standards require it or new standards are issued.

One-on-one training is possibly the most effective training method. The supervisor periodically spends some time watching an individual employee work. Then the supervisor meets with the employee to discuss safe work practices, bestow credit for safe work, and provide additional instruction to counteract any observed unsafe practices. One-on-one training is most effective when applied to all employees under supervision and not just those with whom there appears to be a problem. Positive feedback given for safe work practices is a very powerful tool. It helps workers establish new safe behavior patterns and recognizes and thereby reinforces the desired behavior.

Safety and Health Training for Managers

Training managers is necessary to ensure their continuing support and understanding. It is their responsibility to communicate the program's goals and objectives to their employees, as well as assign safety and health responsibilities, and hold subordinates accountable.

Safety and Health Training for Supervisors

Supervisors may need additional training in hazard detection, accident investigation, their role in ensuring maintenance of controls, emergency handling, and use of personal protective equipment. Supervisors play a critical role in any safety program through their daily contact with workers. Top management shows its commitment by training supervisors to understand their responsibilities for ensuring workplace safety.

Supervisors need to understand the safety and health regulations that apply to their workplace. Consider having your supervisors attend an OSHA 10-hour outreach program that covers many of the more general standards.

Employee Orientation Training

An orientation program should be available to each new employee. This is true for all employment levels management, supervisory, or worker. New employees are usually open to ideas and information about the way business is done. From the first day, new employees begin to formulate opinions about the organization, managers, supervisors, and fellow workers.

The format and extent of orientation training will depend on the complexity of hazards and the work practices needed to control them. An orientation may consist of a quick review of site safety and health rules, hazard communication training, and a run-through of job tasks. Larger workplaces with more complex hazards and work practices to control them, may wish to start with a clear description of hazards, followed by a discussion of how to protect oneself. Employees may have on-the-job training and may shadow an experienced employee for a period of time.

Employee orientation is a good way to provide much of the initial safety and health training that may be required, particularly if participation is mandatory for all employees. If your company already has an orientation for new employees that covers items such as company benefits and work hours, consider including a safety and health training component.

If your company's training matrix contains safety topics that are required for everyone, then these topics are good candidates for orientation. Typically, such topics may include the "Hazard Communication Plan," "Forklift Awareness," or "Lockout Awareness."

New Employee Orientation is a good place to discuss your company's Safety and Health Policy, management's commitment to safety and health, and ways in which employees are encouraged to participate in the training. This is the employee's first opportunity and impression of your organization's safety and health program.

On-the-Job Training

While much safety and health training can be provided in formal, structured formats (lectures, video, classroom, etc.), training may be provided more effectively in small groups or one-on-one within the employee's department. On-the-job training (OJT), as its name implies, occurs within the context of the work environment. A supervisor or other qualified personnel delivers it, often providing opportunities for hands-on practice with close supervision. While the delivery format is generally informal, the content and learning activities should be consistent for all trainees.

On-the-job training can be a good method to deliver content that is specific for a particular department and would not be covered during general employee orientation. For example, supervisors should develop a checklist for OJT topics for their departments, which might include:

- Hazards associated with specific chemicals used in the department;
- Safe usage, handling and maintenance of tools, supplies and equipment (including PPE); and
- Proper procedures for safe performance of tasks and jobs and handling emergencies.

OJT offers opportunities to increase employee participation in the safety program. Seasoned employees with expertise in certain areas can help develop the departmental OJT checklist and ones who perform their jobs in an exemplary manner can help train others.

Refresher Training

No training is complete without follow-up. Monitor employee's progress often during the first months. Have them demonstrate their skills. Answer questions, correct mistakes, and make sure they follow safety procedures. You may want to have a follow-up refresher course for more experienced employees. This will reinforce your safety message once more.

Research shows that when you include safety procedures in new employee training programs, morale improves and the accident rate decreases. First impressions can last throughout a career. Training is an ideal opportunity to make those impressions positive and to teach safe and productive work habits to all employees.

Refresher training is needed for a number of reasons. Some skills may be used infrequently or only on an "as needed" basis [for example, cardiopulmonary resuscitation (CPR)]. Other skills require refresher training if circumstances or the work environment change. For example:

> If a department begins using a new solvent, employees will need hazard communication training on that product.

Finally, some skills may need to be monitored to make sure safe practices continue and that gaps in learning have not occurred. For example, if employees are not completing pre-shift forklift inspections.

Some OSHA standards have specific requirements for refresher training; while others do not. The standards that require refresher training describe what needs to be provided in the training. They also vary with respect to frequency of the training. Some standards require refresher training on a regular basis.

For example, the respiratory protection standard requires it. Others require it only under certain circumstances. Hazard Communication requires it when a new chemical is introduced. Also, if you find there is a need for refresher training, even if OSHA doesn't require it, this is just good practice.

As you determine your OSHA training requirements, note whether or not each standard has a requirement for refresher training. This information is usually included in each standard, generally with the information on training.

Motor Vehicle Safety Training

In 1987, over-the-road motor vehicle accidents were the leading cause of work-related deaths. Given the grim reality of this hazard, all workers operating a motor vehicle on the job should be trained in its safe operation. In 1990 OSHA proposed a standard requiring that such workers wear seat belts and receive safe driving training.

Training in safe loading and unloading practices, safe speed in relation to varying conditions, and proper vehicle maintenance has been found helpful in reducing work-related vehicle injuries. Do not overlook the training of on-premises vehicle drivers. These drivers can be exposed to such hazards as vehicle imbalance, loads tipping while the vehicle is cornering and dangers related to battery charging. We urge you to emphasize in the strongest possible terms the benefits of safe driving and the potentially fatal consequences of unsafe practices.

Personal Protective Equipment (PPE) Training

Supervisors and workers alike must be taught the proper selection, use, and maintenance of PPE. Since PPE sometimes can be cumbersome, employees may need to be motivated to wear it in every situation where protection is necessary. Therefore, training should begin with a clear explanation of why the equipment is necessary, how its use will benefit the wearer and what its limitations are. Remind your employees of your desire to protect them and of your efforts, not only to eliminate and reduce the hazards, but also to provide suitable PPE where needed. Explain how essential it is that they do their part to protect their health and safety.

Individual employees need to become familiar with the PPE they are being asked to wear. This is done by handling it and putting it on. Training consists of showing employees how to put the equipment on, how to wear it properly, and how to test for proper fit. Proper fit is essential if the equipment is to provide the intended protection. It is especially important in the case of negative pressure respirators, so special fit testing is necessary.

The effectiveness of some PPE also depends on proper maintenance. Employees must be trained to maintain the equipment themselves or to see that others maintain it properly. Vendors of the equipment and manufacturers' instructions may be your best sources of maintenance information.

Does your company have employees who do not regularly use PPE, but who will be expected to use it during an emergency response? These employees also must be trained in PPE use, fit, and maintenance. In your overall training program, include simulated emergency training exercises where employees use the equipment. Repeated and even frequent training is often necessary. For example:

Your emergency response plans may call for using self-contained respirators to escape from atmospheres immediately dangerous to life or health. You should conduct frequent exercises in finding, donning and properly using these protective devices. If they ever are needed, you will want your employees capable of responding quickly and knowledgeably.

Expect to repeat the PPE training for new hires, contract workers, and employees in newly assigned jobs.

Emergency Response Training

Train your employees to respond to emergency situations. Every employee at every worksite needs to understand:

- Emergency telephone numbers and who may use them;
- Emergency exits and how they are marked;

- Evacuation routes; and
- Signals that alert employees to the need to evacuate.

In addition, practice evacuation drills at least annually, so that every employee has a chance to recognize the signal and evacuate in a safe and orderly fashion. Supervisors or their alternates should practice counting personnel at evacuation gathering points to ensure that every worker is accounted for.

Do not forget anyone at your site when you are practicing for emergencies. You should have procedures to account for visitors, contract employees, and service workers such as cafeteria employees. One effective practice technique is secretly to have one or two employees simulate an injury or other immobilizing problem during an evacuation drill.

They could, for instance, slip away to a stairwell not on the evacuation route and there await discovery and rescue. Such an experience can demonstrate forcefully to your supervisors and alternates the importance of an accurate count.

Additional special instruction and drilling may be necessary at sites where weather or earthquake emergencies are reasonable possibilities. For example, where there is a good chance of tornadoes, employees should learn to distinguish the signals for evacuation and for taking shelter and should practice responses to both.

If you have established emergency response teams at your workplace, all members of these teams are covered by OSHA's Bloodborne Pathogens standard (Part 1910.1030 of Title 29 of the Code of Federal Regulations), which includes training requirements.

Training for Spanish-Speaking Employees

Employers are hiring a growing number of Hispanic

workers and demanding bilingual job safety and health training. Job training for limited-English Hispanic workers in many workplaces often have problems with job safety training.

The trainer, usually a native English speaker without bilingual skills, grabs a native Spanish speaker with some English skills from the group of workers, and uses this person as an interpreter.

The training begins with the trainer speaking through the interpreter. Sometime during the training session, the trainer asks the trainees if there are any questions. The trainees hardly ever have any questions. The training ends with the trainer asking the trainees if they understood everything. The trainees nod their heads in a "yes" motion, indicating they understood everything. Guess what? They didn't.

Safety training for Spanish speaking employees can pay big dividends. This hands-on training approach is also recognized by OSHA.

From both construction sites to manufacturing plants, America's blue-collar work force stands as a testament to diversity and the Spanish speaking population is being left behind because employers are neglecting to train them.

Smart employers, however, are learning that cultural sensitivity has much deeper meaning than previously thought. By truly understanding and respecting the literacy, cultural and language differences of their workers, companies can gain financially while creating a safer work environment for employees.

Perhaps most importantly, by tailoring training programs to fit the needs of individual employees, companies decrease injury rates, increase work force productivity, promote loyalty and lower insurance expenses.

Businesses have come to accept the simple truth that worker training pays big dividends. But when faced with the task of providing classes for illiterate or Spanish-speaking workers, even the most committed employers sometimes shrink from the responsibility to train.

These workers, however, often are the ones who most desperately need training. That is why OSHA launched a campaign to better protect non-English-speaking workers, who are considered to be at high risk of on-the-job injury. OSHA recognized that more than 10 million Americans speak little or no English and one in five Americans does not speak English at home.

In the Hispanic population, for example, numbers from the Bureau of Labor Statistics show that the fatality rate for Hispanic employees climbed by more than 11 percent in 2000, while deaths for all other groups declined. OSHA attributed this increase, at least in part, to the language barrier.

Aside from the statistics on injuries and death, poor training for Spanish-speaking workers also results in low productivity, high turnover and other expenses for their employers.

While some employers recognize these statistics, almost none fully understand the importance of cultural differences in the workplace. A large portion of America's non-skilled and semi-skilled labor has immigrated from Mexico and other countries. They bring with them a set of beliefs regarding work ethic, family, and company loyalty. Only by understanding and reacting positively to these beliefs can an employer maximize the productivity of workers from other cultures.

Another challenge lies in training semi-literate workers, many of whom speak English as their first language. These workers lack the learning style and reading abilities that many employers assume they have.

For these businesses, the answer may lie in a new method of worker training. This method combines the obvious benefits of teaching workers in their first languages with the improved results of a hands-on, practice-makes-perfect approach. Plus, this culturally intensive training includes sessions for supervisors and managers, helping them to understand and respect their employees.

Hands-on Training

The very nature of training and safety programs makes it difficult to measure return-on-investment. After all, how can a company determine the number of accidents that would have happened without training, as well as the human and financial costs of these incidents?

But at one of the largest municipal construction projects in the Dallas area, evidence has emerged to confirm the value of a bilingual, hands-on work safety program.

For example, the workers on the project are required to attend 40 hours of training in basic occupational safety and health procedures. Nearly 8,000 of the project's workers have been trained during the last two years, with sessions conducted in both English and Spanish. Perhaps most importantly, the training features a culturally sensitive, hands-on approach that engages workers, helping them learn new skills to apply in their day-to-day jobs.

Compared to a national average of 3.9 injuries per 200,000 man-hours, this project has seen only 0.3 injuries. As a result, only $600,000 in workers' compensation claims have been made against the $2.6 million that managers expected to spend in the first year of the project.

Perhaps the clearest evidence of the training program's success shows up in the average cost of worker's compensation claims. The average claim per worker trained has totaled $1,500, versus $10,000 for those who were not trained. In the final analysis, lives and millions of dollars have been saved.

Classroom Training

Traditionally, training for employees consisted of lectures, videos and other classroom-based methods. This approach often has little impact on workers who are not native English speakers. And they are not the only ones. Workers in low-skilled and semi-skilled jobs typically have low literacy rates no matter what their cultural backgrounds.

While the audio-visual approach may work with mid-level managers, unskilled and semi-skilled employees work with their hands to create a living. So it stands to reason that they would best receive training in a hands-on environment. After the instructor demonstrates a skill, each worker must successfully duplicate the instructor's technique. And if the students do not succeed at their first effort, they must continue trying until they get it right. This outcome-based approach ensures each employee truly understands how to safely and correctly perform his or her duties.

The approach also improves the relationship between English-speaking and non-English-speaking workers. Training classes are conducted in English and Spanish. Everyone from front-line construction workers to project managers and company owners attended the same sessions.

This hands-on approach creates a sense of trust and respect between classmates. As a result, Spanish-speaking workers who might not have openly questioned their supervisors in the past were given the tools and encouragement to speak up when they saw potential safety hazards.

English-speaking workers also developed a stronger sense of confidence in their non-English-speaking colleagues, since everybody had the same level of safety training.

Savings in Financial Terms

Workers who are trained up-front in their primary languages and with sensitivity to their cultures bring a slew of benefits to their employers. But training is just a first step. Employers also must put workers in their comfort zone, surrounding them with people of their own culture. This frees them to speak up among the group, asking for help and information.

The rewards can be very significant, both in financial and human terms. First and foremost, these employees suffer fewer injuries. This reduces workers' compensation claims, as well as the overall cost of insurance premiums, damaged equipment, wasted raw materials, and pain and suffering.

Well-trained employees also vastly increase their productivity. With formal instruction, they avoid picking up the bad habits of other workers who might demonstrate less-desirable work techniques. And no matter what their language, well-trained workers are more likely to stick around, reducing turnover and costs.

These benefits can be gained by companies of all sizes. While in-house training is more common in larger companies, it can actually be of greater importance to smaller businesses. These smaller companies have fewer resources to withstand the negative financial impact of a large workers' compensation claim, lawsuit or boosted insurance premiums. To guard against these losses, smaller businesses should focus a greater amount of time and attention on training their workers for health and safety.

Bilingual Training

Companies faced with the challenge of overcoming

language, cultural and literacy barriers should look for training providers that offer:

- Programs that are recognized by OSHA as a National Best Practice;
- Bilingual classes that address cultural issues; and
- Training programs that minimize literacy requirements.

Companies must take immediate steps to provide appropriate training either in-house or through qualified training providers and protect their employees. In return, employers will be rewarded with increased productivity, lower turnover and reduced costs.

Those companies choosing not to properly train their employees because of language, literacy and cultural barriers risk paying a price they cannot afford, in both dollars and lives.

CHAPTER 3:

HOW TO DEVELOP AN EFFECTIVE TRAINING PROGRAM

Managers who are responsible for training have many other duties and functions unrelated to safety training. In many cases, the safety and health staff are responsible for company training programs. Many do not have the background, time, and resources to design and implement training programs that meet OSHA's regulatory requirements.

More and more, companies are questioning their investment in employee training programs. They see growing expenditures with no direct tie-in to the bottom line. Often, when companies are faced with the need to reduce costs, training is high on the list of areas to cut.

At the same time, employees face an ever-increasing array of training options.

Part of a training manager's job is to help employees set their learning agendas. You want to make sure that employees spend time and resources gaining skills and knowledge that will benefit them *and* be of value to the company. Training managers must typically face in two directions at once:

- Towards management, to understand company training needs, encourage corporate support, and keep leaders informed about training programs; and
- Towards the employees, to help plan how they can contribute to company needs while satisfying their own learning goals.

Assess Current Training Programs

Hopefully you won't have to start from scratch; it's likely that your company has some kind of training in place already even if it's ad hoc and informal. Look at what is there, particularly:

- How well-trained are employees at all levels?
- What process is in place to propose and approve training?
- What methods are used to train and develop employees?
- What overall priority is training given, and what resources are set aside for it?

Produce a Training Plan

It's essential to have a written training plan before you begin working with employees on their learning agendas. A written plan serves two purposes:

First, it's a document that you can share with management. A commitment from management to support training is crucial to the success of the program, and managers need to know what they're committing to. You're a lot more likely to succeed when your plan is reviewed and approved by company leaders; and

Second, it's a benchmark for measuring the effectiveness of training activities. With a written plan, you can assess the original plan against what is actually happening, and also gauge the quality of the training and the benefits that result.

You may want to address the following in your plan:

- The process for identifying and assessing individual training needs;
- How employees will be trained and developed within the organization; and
- Available resources, including financial.

Sample Safety and Health Training Plan

_____ (Company Name)

Introduction

Training is one of the most important elements in our company's Safety and Health Program. It gives employees an opportunity to learn their jobs properly bring new ideas into the workplace, reinforce existing ideas and practices, and put our Safety and Health Program into action.

Everyone in our company will benefit from safety and health training through fewer workplace injuries and illnesses, reduced stress, and higher morale. Productivity, profits, and competitiveness will increase as production costs per unit, turnover, and workers compensation rates lower.

Management Commitment

_____ will provide the necessary funds and scheduling time to ensure effective safety and health training is provided. This commitment will include paid work time for training and training in the language that the worker understands. Both management and employees will be involved in developing the program.

To most effectively carry out their safety responsibilities, all employees must understand their role in that program, the hazards, and potential hazards that need to be prevented or controlled, and the ways to protect themselves and others. We will achieve these goals by:

- Educate all managers, supervisors, and employees on their safety management system responsibilities;
- Educate all employees about the specific hazards and control measures in their workplace;
- Train all employees on hazard identification,

analysis, reporting, and control procedures; and
- Train all employees on safe work procedures.

Our training program will focus on health and safety concerns that determine the best way to deal with a particular hazard. When a hazard is identified we will first try to remove it entirely. If that is not feasible, we will then train workers to protect themselves, if necessary, against the remaining hazard.

Once we have decided that a safety or health problem can best be addressed by training (or by another method combined with training) we will follow up by developing specific training goals based on those particular needs.

Employees. At a minimum, employees must know the general safety and health rules of the worksite specific site hazards and the safe work practices needed to help control exposure, and the individual's role in all types of emergency situations. We will ensure all employees understand the hazards to which they may be exposed and how to prevent harm to themselves and others from exposure to these hazards.

We will commit available resources to ensure employees receive safety and health training during the following:

- Whenever a person is hired general safety orientation including an overview of company safety rules, and why those rules must be followed.
- Whenever an employee is given a new job assignment during formal classroom training, and again, when the supervisor provides specific task training. It's extremely important that supervisors emphasize safety during initial task assignment.
- Whenever new work procedures are begun during formal classroom training and supervisor on the-job training.
- Whenever new equipment is installed if new hazards are introduced.

- Whenever new substances are used hazard communication program may apply.
- The bottom line train safety whenever a new hazard is introduced to the employee.

Employees

Employees must know they are responsible for complying with all company safety rules, and that most accidents will be prevented by their safe work practices. They must be very familiar with any personal protective equipment required for their jobs. They must know what to do in case of emergencies.

Each employee needs to understand that they are not expected to start working a new assignment until they have been properly trained. If a job appears to be unsafe, they will report the situation to their supervisor.

Supervisors

Supervisors will be given special training to help them in their leadership role. They need to be taught to look for hidden hazards in the work under their supervision, to insist upon the maintenance of the physical protection in their areas, and to reinforce employee hazard training through performance feedback and, when necessary, fair and consistent enforcement. We will commit necessary resources to ensure supervisors understand the following responsibilities and the reasons for them:

- Detecting and correcting hazards in their work areas before they result in injuries or illnesses;
- Providing physical resources and psychosocial support that promote safe work;
- Providing performance feedback and effective recognition and discipline techniques; and
- Conducting on-the-job training.

Supervisors are considered the primary safety trainers. All

supervisors will complete train-the-trainer classes to learn training techniques and how to test employee knowledge and skills. They will also receive training on how to apply fair and consistent recognition and discipline. Supervisor training may be provided by the supervisor's immediate manager, by the Safety Department, or by outside resources.

Managers

All line managers must understand their responsibilities within our Safety and Health Program. This may require classroom training and other forms of communication that ensure that managers understand their safety and health responsibilities. Formal classroom training may not be necessary. The subject can be covered periodically as a part of regular management meetings.

Managers will be Trained in the Following Subject Areas:

- The elements of the safety management system, and the positive impact of the various processes within the system can have on corporate objectives.

- Their responsibility to communicate the Safety and Health Program goals and objectives to their employees.

- Their role also includes making clear assignments of Safety and Health Program responsibilities, providing authority and resources to carry out assigned tasks, and holding subordinate managers and supervisors accountable.

- Actively requiring compliance with mandatory Safety and Health Program policies and rules and encouraging employee involvement in discretionary safety activities such as making suggestions and participation in the safety committee.

Training will emphasize the importance of managers' visibly showing their commitment to the safety and health program. They will be expected to set a good example by scrupulously following all the safety and health rules themselves.

Recognition and Reward

The purpose of an effective system of recognition is to motivate employee involvement and build ownership in our safety system. When employees make suggestions that will improve our safety training, we will recognize them. When employees make a significant contribution to the success of the company we will recognize and reward their performance. Employees will submit all suggestions directly to immediate supervisors. Supervisors are authorized to reward employees on-the-spot when the suggestion substantially improves the training process or content.

Training and Accountability

To help make sure our efforts in safety and health are effective we have developed methods to measure performance and administer consequences. Managers must understand that they have a responsibility to first meet their obligations to our employees prior to administering any discipline for violating safety policies and rules.

Managers and safety staff will be educated on the following elements (processes) of the safety accountability system. They will be trained on the procedures to evaluate and improve these elements.

Training will focus on improving the Safety and Health Program whenever hazardous conditions and unsafe or inappropriate behaviors are detected. At the same time, we will use effective education and training to establish a strong "culture of accountability."

Safety orientation will emphasize that compliance with safety policies, procedures, and rules as outlined in the safety plan is a condition of employment. Discipline will be administered to help the employee increase desired behaviors, not to in any way punish. Safety accountability will be addressed at every training session.

Types of Training

Required rules-related training will be conducted according to OSHA Regulations. We will also make sure additional training is conducted as deemed appropriate.

_____ (Responsible individual) will ensure Safety and Health Program training is in full compliance with OSHA standards.

New Employee Orientation

The format and extent of orientation training will depend on the complexity of hazards and the work practices needed to control them. Orientation will include a combination of initial classroom and follow-up on-the-job training.

- For some jobs, orientation may consist of a quick review of site safety and health rules; hazard communication training for the toxic substances present at the site; training required by relevant OSHA standards, e.g., fire protection, lockout/tagout, etc; and a run-through of the job tasks. This training be presented by the new employee's supervisor or delegated employee.

- For larger tasks with more complex hazards and work practices to control them, orientation will be structured carefully. We will make sure that our new employees start the job with a clear understanding of the hazards and how to protect themselves and others.

We will follow up supervisory training with a buddy system, where a worker with lengthy experience is assigned to watch over and coach a new worker, either for a set period of time or until it is determined that training is complete.

Whether the orientation is brief or lengthy, the supervisor will make sure that before new employees begin the job, they receive instruction in responding to emergencies. All orientation training received will be properly documented.

Contract Workers

Will receive training to recognize our specific workplace's hazards or potential hazards.

Experienced Workers

Will be trained if the installation of new equipment changes their job in any way, or if process changes create new hazards or increase previously existing hazards.

All workers will receive refresher training as necessary to keep them prepared for emergencies and alert to ongoing housekeeping problems.

Personal Protective Equipment (PPE)

Workers needing to wear personal protective equipment (PPE) and persons working in high risk situations will need special training. Supervisors and workers alike must be taught the proper selection, use, and maintenance of PPE. Since PPE sometimes can be cumbersome, employees may need to be motivated to wear it in every situation where protection is necessary. Therefore, training will begin with a clear explanation of why the equipment is necessary, how its use will benefit the wearer, and what its limitations are. Remind your employees of your desire to protect them and of your efforts, not only to eliminate and reduce the hazards, but also to provide suitable PPE where needed.

Individual employees will become familiar with the PPE they are being asked to wear. This is done by handling it and putting it on. Training will consist of showing employees how to put the equipment on, how to wear it properly, and how to test for proper fit and how to maintain it. Proper fit is essential if the equipment is to provide the intended protection. We will conduct periodic exercises in finding, donning, and properly using emergency personal protective equipment and devices.

Vehicular Safety

All workers operating a motor vehicle on the job (on or off premises) will be trained in its safe vehicle operation, safe loading and unloading practices, safe speed in relation to varying conditions, and proper vehicle maintenance. We will emphasize in the strongest possible terms the benefits of safe driving and the potentially fatal consequences of unsafe practices.

Emergency Response

We will train our employees to respond to emergency situations. Every employee at every worksite will understand:

- Emergency telephone numbers and who may use them;
- Emergency exits and how they are marked;
- Evacuation routes; and
- Signals that alert employees to the need to evacuate.

We will practice evacuation drills at least semi-annually, so that every employee has a chance to recognize the signal and evacuate in a safe and orderly fashion. Supervisors or their alternates will practice counting personnel at evacuation gathering points to ensure that every worker is accounted for.

We will include procedures to account for visitors, contract employees, and service workers such as cafeteria employees. At sites where weather or earthquake emergencies are reasonable possibilities, additional special instruction, and drilling will be given.

Periodic Safety and Health Training

At some worksites, complex work practices are necessary to control hazards. Elsewhere, occupational injuries and illness are common. At such sites, we will ensure that employees receive periodic safety and health training to refresh their memories and to teach new methods of control. New training also will also be conducted as necessary when OSHA standards change or new standards are issued.

Where the work situation changes rapidly, weekly meetings will be conducted needed. These meetings will remind workers of the upcoming week's tasks, the environmental changes that may affect them, and the procedures they may need to protect themselves and others.

Identifying Types of Training

Specific hazards that employees need to know about should be identified through total site health and safety surveys, job hazard analysis, and change analysis. Company accident and injury records may reveal additional hazards and needs for training. Near-miss reports, maintenance requests, and employee suggestions may uncover still other hazards requiring employee training.

Safety and Health Training Program Evaluation

We will determine whether the training provided has

achieved its goal of improving employee safety performance. Evaluation will highlight training program strengths and identify areas of weakness that need change or improvement.

_____(The safety committee/coordinator) will evaluate training through the following methods:

- Observation of employee skills.
- Surveys and interviews to determine employee knowledge and attitudes about training.
- Review of the training plan and lesson plans.
- Comparing training conducted with hazards in the workplace.
- Review of training documents.
- Compare pre- and post-training injury and accident rates.

If evaluation determines program improvement is necessary, the safety committee/coordinator will development recommendations.

Certification

_____

_____

Reviewed by (Signature) Date

_____

_____

Approved by (Signature) Date

Teaching and Learning Principles

Training our supervisors and employees need not be complex or lengthy. Five basic principles will guide our Safety and Health Training Program:

- *Perceived Purpose:* The trainee must understand the purpose of the instruction. Therefore, the beginning of any training program should focus on why this instruction will be useful.

- *Order of Presentation:* Information should be organized to maximize understanding. For example, if we are teaching employees the proper way to use a respirator, the order in which we present the material should match the steps the employee must use to choose, fit, wear, and maintain the respirator.

- *Appropriate Practice:* We learn best when we can immediately practice and apply newly acquired knowledge and skills. Therefore, job safety and health instruction is best given at the worksite where demonstration, practice, and application can be immediate. When onsite instruction is not feasible, arrange for our employees to practice and apply the new knowledge and skills as soon as possible.

- *Knowledge of Results:* As we practice, we need to know as soon as possible if we are correct. Practicing a task incorrectly can lead to harmful patterns. Praise for correct actions enhances motivation and encourages formation of desirable habits.

- *Individual Differences:* We are individuals, and we learn in different ways. A successful training program incorporates a variety of learning opportunities, such as written instruction, audio-visual instruction, lectures, and hands-on coaching. Also, we learn at different speeds. The pace of the training should recognize these differences. One effective way to learn is by teaching others. Therefore, after the initial instruction and some practice, it can be very helpful to divide the group into teacher/learner teams, sometimes pairing a rapid learner with a slower one, but also giving the slower learner a chance to teach.

Developing Learning Activities

We will develop our learning activities to meet the training needs we have identified by employing the five learning principles described above. We need to be imaginative in our choice of methods and materials, and make full use of our resources. One way to get ideas is by looking at the training programs of companies in our industry.

Conducting Training

If our employees are to learn and to improve, they must feel motivated. Here are some suggestions for enhancing the success of your safety and health training:

- Prepare employees for training by putting them at ease.
- Recruit employees who show signs of being good trainers of their coworkers. Prepare them to conduct this peer training.
- Explain the job or training topic. Determine how much your employees already know about it.
- Boost your employees' interest in training by helping them understand its benefits. For example, training can reduce injuries and near-misses, and training can enhance productivity and overall job performance, thereby improving the chance for advancement and other rewards.
- Pace the instruction to the trainees' learning speed. Present the material clearly and patiently.
- Present only as much information in one session as your employees can master.
- Have your employees perform each step of the operation and repeat your instructions and explanations. Have them repeat a task until you are satisfied they know how to do it.
- Encourage employees to help each other by dividing the group into teacher/learner pairs or practice pairs.
- Check frequently for correct performance during the

initial practice period. Taper off on surveillance as the trainees become more proficient.

- Encourage your employees to build the new skill into the way they work best, but caution them not to change the newly learned procedure without first checking with you or their supervisor.

Definitions

Certified indicates that a worker has successfully completed specialized training and that the training has been certified in writing by a professional organization. For example, OSHA's safety and health rules allow only trained audiologists, otolaryngologists, or technicians who have been certified by the Council of Accreditation in Occupational Hearing Conservation to perform audiometric tests.

Designated generally refers to a person who has received extensive training in a particular task and is assigned by the employer to per for m that task in specific operations.

Authorized refers to a person permitted by an employer to be in a regulated area; the term also refers to a person assigned by an employer to perform a specific task or to be in a specific location at a jobsite.

Competent person is someone who has broad knowledge of worksite safety and health issues, who is capable of identifying existing and predictable worksite hazards, and who has management approval to control the hazards. Only a competent person can supervise erecting, moving, or dismantling scaffolds at a worksite, for example.

On-the-job training is possibly the most effective training method. The supervisor periodically spends some time watching an individual employee work. Then he/she meets with the employee to discuss safe work practices, bestow credit for safe work, and provide additional instruction to counteract any observed unsafe practices.

One-on-one training is most effective when applied to all employees under supervision and not just those with whom there appears to be a problem. This is because the positive feedback given for safe work practices is this method's most powerful tool. It helps workers establish new safe behavior patterns. It also recognizes and thereby reinforces the desired behavior.

Qualified person is someone who, through training and professional experience, has demonstrated the ability to resolve problems relating to a specific task or process. For example, an individual may be qualified to perform electrical circuit tests but not qualified to perform hydraulic pressure tests.

Safety Training Most Frequently Asked Questions (FAQ's)

QUESTION: How do we determine the need for safety training?

ANSWER: Safety training does not simply involve inviting a group of workers to a meeting on the safety topic of the month. It involves planning, preparation or development, and evaluation. But even before you get to the planning point of your program, you need to do some preliminary legwork, or analysis, to determine when training is the appropriate organizational response to a problem, issue, or need. So, before you commit to a training program, analyze organizational needs and specific problems, and review regulatory requirements for training.

Safety and health training should be provided before problems or accidents occur. This training would cover both general safety and health rules and work procedures and would be repeated if an accident or near miss incident occurs.

Problems that can be addressed effectively by training include those that arise from a lack of knowledge of a work process, unfamiliarity with equipment, or incorrect execution of a task. Training is less effective (but still can be used) for problems arising from an employee's lack of motivation or lack of attention to the job. Whatever its purpose, training is most effective when designed in relation to the goals of the employer's total safety and health program.

QUESTION: What is considered proper training under OSHA's Hazard Communication standard?

ANSWER: The training provisions of the Hazard Communication standard (HCS) 29 CFR 1910.1200 are not satisfied solely by giving employee the MSDS to read. An employer's training program is to be a forum for explaining to employees not only the hazards of the chemicals in their work area, but also how to use the information generated in the hazard communication program.

This can be accomplished in many ways (audiovisuals, classroom instruction, interactive video), and should include an opportunity for employees to ask questions to ensure that they understand the information presented to them. Training need not be conducted on each specific chemical found in the workplace, but may be conducted by categories of hazard (e.g., carcinogens, sensitizers, acutely toxic agents) that are or may be encountered by an employee during the course of his duties. Furthermore, the training must be comprehensible. If the employees receive job instructions in a language other than English, then the training and information to be conveyed under the HCS will also need to be conducted in a foreign language.

QUESTION: How often does an employee have to be trained in Hazard Communication or Right-To-Know (HazCom)?

ANSWER: OSHA's training requirements are found at 29 CFR 1910.1200(h). At 1910.1200(h)(1), it states: "Employers shall provide employees with effective information and training on hazardous chemicals n their work area at the time of their initial assignment, and whenever a new physical or health hazard the employees have not previously been trained about is introduced into their work area."

QUESTION: Does OSHA require any type of training when employees operate forklift trucks?

ANSWER: The standard requires employers to develop and implement a training program based on the general principles of safe truck operation, the types of vehicle(s) being used in the workplace, the hazards of the workplace created by the use of the vehicle(s), and the general safety requirements of the OSHA standard.

Trained operators must know how to do the job properly and do it safely as demonstrated by workplace evaluation. Formal (lecture, video, etc.) and practical (demonstration and practical exercises) training must be provided. Employers must also certify that each operator has received the training and evaluate each operator at least once every three years.

Prior to operating the truck in the workplace, the employer must evaluate the operator's performance and determine the operator to be competent to operate a powered industrial truck safely. Refresher training is needed whenever an operator demonstrates a deficiency in the safe operation of the truck.

QUESTION: How much forklift training does OSHA require for new and temporary employees who have previously operated forklift vehicles?

ANSWER: Employers employing new operators or temporary labor operators who claim prior training must evaluate the applicability and adequacy of prior training to determine if all required training topics have been covered. Factors to consider include the following:

- The type of equipment operated;
- Amount of experience on that equipment;
- How recent was this experience; and
- The type of environment in which the operator worked.

The employer may, but is not required to, use written documentation of the earlier training to determine whether an operator has been properly trained.

The operator's competency may also simply be evaluated by the employer or another person with the requisite knowledge, skills, and experience to perform evaluations. The employer can determine from this information whether the experience is recent and thorough enough, and whether the operator has demonstrated sufficient competence in operating in the powered industrial truck to forego any or some of the initial training. Some training on site regarding specific factors of the new operator's workplace is likely always to be necessary.

Under the OSHA multi-employer worksite policy, citations may be issued to employers using temporary employees as forklift operators. A warehouse employer who supervises temporary employees would have the responsibility to ensure safe powered industrial truck operations.

A temporary employee involved in an instance of unsafe operation, an accident, or a near-miss incident at a warehouse employer's worksite would require refresher training before being allowed to resume driving a forklift vehicle.

QUESTION: What information can I use to help train employees to deal with heat?

ANSWER: Heat stress is an occupational health issue that requires emphasis in work environments. Employers who have employees directly affected by hot work environments must take precautions to prevent heat stress from occurring. Instruct employees to follow good work practices after you have done what you can to:

- Actually cool the work environment;
- Provide longer rest periods during the day;
- Acclimatize workers to the heat.

Employee education is vital to make workers aware of the need to replace fluids and salt lost through sweat. In addition, they should be able to recognize the following heat disorders:

- Dehydration
- Exhaustion
- Fainting
- Heat cramps salt deficiency
- Heat exhaustion
- Heat stroke

QUESTION: Is there a list of OSHA's Training requirements?

ANSWER: The following are OSHA's training requirements for both General Industry 29 CFR Part 1910 Standards, and Construction Industry 29 CFR Part 1926 Standards listed alphabetically.

OSHA STANDARDS	OSHA'S Required Training Standards
1910.25	Portable wood ladders
1926.26	Portable metal ladders
1910.27	Fixed ladders
1910.28	Safety requirements for scaffolding
1910.38	Emergency action plans
1910.66	Powered platforms
1910.67	Vehicle-mounted elevating and rotating platforms
1910.68	Manlifts
1910.95	Occupational noise exposure
1910.106	Flammable & combustible liquids
1910.109	Explosives & blasting agents
1910.110	Storage & handling of liquefied petroleum gases
1910.111	Storage & handling of anhydrous ammonia
1910.119	Process safety management of highly hazardous chemicals
1910.120	Hazardous waste operations and emergency response
1904.133	Eye and face protection
1910.134	Respiratory protection
1910.135	Head protection
1910.136	Foot protection
1910.138	Hand protection
1910.145	Accident prevention signs & tags

1910.146	Permit-required confined spaces
1910.147	Lockout/tagout
1910.151	Medical services & first aid
1910.156	Fire brigades
1910.157	Portable fire extinguishers
1910.160	Fixed extinguishing systems
1910.164	Fire detection systems
1910.165	Fire alarm systems
1910.177	Servicing multi-piece & single rim wheels
1910.178	Powered industrial trucks
1910.179	Overhead & gantry cranes
1910.180	Crawler locomotive & truck cranes
1910.181	Derricks
1910.217	Mechanical power presses
1910.218	Forging machines
1910.252	Welding, cutting & brazing
1910.261	Pulp, paper & paperboard mills
1910.264	Laundry machinery & operations
1910.266	Logging
1910.268	Telecommunications
1910.269	Electrical power generation, transmission & distribution
1910.272	Grain handling
1910.331-335	Electrical
1910.410	Commercial diving

1910.1001	Asbestos
1910.1003 - 1016	Toxic & hazardous substances
1910.1018	Inorganic arsenic
1910.1025	Lead
1910.1027	Cadmium
1910.1028	Benzene
1910.1029	Coke oven emissions
1910.1030	Bloodborne pathogens
1910.1043	Cotton dust
1910.1044	1,2-Dibromo-3-Chloropropane
1910.1045	Acrylonitrile
1910.1047	Ethylene oxide
1910.1048	Formaldehyde
1910.1050	Methylenedianiline (MDA)
1910.1051	1, 3 Butadiene
1910.1052	Methylene chloride
1910.1096	Ionizing radiation
1910.1200	Hazard communication
1910.1450	Hazardous chemicals in laboratories
1926.20	Safety & health
1926.21	Safety training & education
1926.35	Emergency action plan
1926.50	Medical services & first aid
1926.52	Occupational noise exposure
1926.54	Nonionizing radiation

1926.57	Ventilation
1926.59	Hazard communication
1926.60	Methylenedianiline (MDA)
1926.62	Lead
1926.64	Process safety management of highly hazardous chemicals
1926.65	Hazardous waste operations and emergency response
1926.103	Respiratory protection
1926.150	Fire protection
1926.152	Flammable & combustible liquids
1926.302	Power operated hand tools
1926.304	Woodworking tools
1926.350	Gas welding & cutting
1926.351	Arc welding & cutting
1926.352	Fire prevention
1926.404	Wiring design & protection
1926.453	Aerial lifts
1926.454	Scaffolds
1926.503	Fall protection
1926.550	Cranes & derricks
1926.552	Material hoists
1926.602	Material handling equipment
1926.651	Excavation
1926.652	Protective systems
1926.761	Steel rrection

1926.800	Underground construction
1926.803	Compressed air
1926.901	Blasting & use of explosives
1926.955	Overhead lines
1926.956	Underground lines
1926.1060	Stairways & ladders
1926.1076	Commercial diving
1926.1101	Steel erection
1926.1103-1116	Toxic & hazardous substances
1926.1117	Vinyl chloride
1926.1118	Inorganic arsenic
1926.1127	Cadmium
1926.1128	Benzene
1926.1129	Coke oven emissions
1926.1144	1,2-Dibromo-3-Chloropropane
1926.1145	Acrylonitrile
1926.1147	Ethylene oxide
1926.1148	Formaldehyde
1926.1152	Methylene chloride

QUESTION: How long does our company have to retain records for employee training?

ANSWER: There is no one standard length of time to keep training records for all OSHA regulations. Unlike employee exposure records that must be retained for 30 years and medical records that must be retained for the time of employment plus thirty years (under 29 CFR

1910.1020), training record retention varies from regulation to regulation.

When training records are required, it would be best to always have them available. Consider keeping all training records during the worker's full period of employment. Your company may even set a policy to retain training records for a period after employment has been terminated.

Here are some examples:

- *29 CFR 1910.1030-Bloodborne pathogens-* requires retraining at least annually and a written training record that must be retained for 3 years.
- *29 CFR 1910.134-Respiratory protection-*requires retraining at least annually, but no specific written training record is required. Written fit testing records must be retained until the next test takes place.
- *29 CFR 1910.119-Process safety management-* requires retraining at least every 3 years and a written training record. No training record retention time is specified.
- *29 CFR 1910.1200-Hazard communication-* requires retraining as new hazards are introduced, but no specific written training record is required.
- *29 CFR 1910.132-General requirements for personal protective equipment-*requires retraining as necessary and a written training certification. No training record retention time is specified.
- *29 CFR 1910.147-Lockout/tagout-*requires retraining as necessary and a written training certification. No training record retention time is specified.
- *29 CFR 1910.146-Permit-required confined spaces-*requires retraining as necessary and a written training certification. No training record retention time is specified. Cancelled entry

- permits are required to be retained for 1 year.
- *29 CFR 1910.178-Powered industrial trucks-* requires an operator evaluation at least once every three years and a written training and evaluation certification. No training or evaluation record retention time is specified.

QUESTION: How can our company design a training program for our employees?

ANSWER: While all employees can benefit from safety training, special attention should be given to the training of supervisors, trainers, and workers. In some places, employees and supervisors directly responsible for safety matters need to have certification, as required by the law. The supervisor is generally responsible for much of the training of workers.

Occasions when employee training may be required are:

- Beginning of employment
- Reassignment or transfer to a new job
- Introduction of new equipment, processes, or procedures

All instructors should be taught how to proceed when training a new or inexperienced employee:

- Plan the session beforehand; break the job down into steps; have training aids available
- Explain what is to be done
- Describe all the hazards and protective measures
- Demonstrate each step, stress key points, and answer any questions
- Have the employee carry out each step, correct errors, and compliment good performance

Check frequently after the employee is working independently to ensure correct performance.

QUESTION: What Safety Training does OSHA require annually?

ANSWER: The following federal OSHA general industry 29 CFR 1910 rules include annual retraining of employee:

- Access to employee exposure and medical records - 29 CFR 1910.1020
- Bloodborne pathogens - 29 CFR 1910.1030
- Fire Brigades - 29 CFR 1910.156
- Fixed Extinguishing Systems - 29 CFR 1910.160
- Grain Handling Facilities - 29 CFR 1910.272
- HAZWOPER - 29 CFR 1910.120
- Mechanical Power Presses - 29 CFR 1910.217
- Occupational Noise - 29 CFR 1910.95
- Permit-required confined space - 29 CFR 1910.146
- Portable Fire Extinguishers - 29 CFR 1910.157
- Respiratory protection - 29 CFR 1910.134

QUESTION: Are videos effective for training employees?

ANSWER: Trainees do benefit from watching videos. But, you should not just plug in a video and leave the trainees. You must be involved to get the most from a video. When a video shows something being done differently from your operations, point it out to the viewers and explain why your facility does it differently. Take time to stop the video to make a point or to ask a question. After the video, ask the employees to give workplace–specific examples to lead into the rest of your training session.

A good training video has some advantages over lectures, overheads, or flipcharts:

- Videos can show examples that would otherwise be too complicated, time consuming, or hazardous to demonstrate.

- Videos provide a good overview of the subject, making it easier for you to start with individualized, worksite specific, or in-depth training.
- Videos are from the "outside" world. When employees hear information from an authority other than their in-house trainer, the material has additional credibility.
- Good videos organize the information, summarize it, and highlight the main points to reinforce learning.
- Videos are ready-to-use, standardized resources that can get the same message across over and over again. When someone needs refresher training, a second look at a video serves to refresh the memory.
- Videos can be a gentle, familiar introduction to safety training for new hires. Videos can relieve the tension of the first few hours or days in a new environment where the new trainee is subjected to endless lectures, handbooks, and forms.

QUESTION: Are employers required to have employees' signatures on file for OSHA mandated training?

ANSWER: It is a common industry practice to take attendance of all employees who attended training sessions; however, OSHA does not require signatures from employees who have attended training sessions. Some OSHA standards, such as the Personal Protective Equipment standard, 29 CFR 1910.132, require verification, through a written certification, that each affected employee has received and understood the required training. The written certification must contain the name of each employee trained, the date(s) of training, and identify the subject of the certification.

QUESTION: Does OSHA require an employer to have an employee trained to render first aid?

ANSWER: Yes. The OSHA requirement at 29 CFR 1910.151(b) states, "In the absence of an infirmary, clinic, or hospital in near proximity to the workplace which is used for the treatment of all injured employees, a person or persons shall be adequately trained to render first aid."

QUESTION: How should a company address new employee safety orientation training?

ANSWER: You know how important safety is to new employees, but you have to make them realize it before they face the hazards in your workplace. Make sure you spend some time with new hires on their first day.

First, you need to get their attention. Satisfy their curiosity about their new job by taking them on an in-depth tour of their work areas. This lets you give them a good first impression of the job's hazards and the importance of the protective measures that are in place.

Back in the classroom, start your training with important "need to know" topics. Training on the facility's Emergency Action Plan, how to report injuries or hazards, warning signs, the hazard communication program, personal protective equipment (PPE), and/or lifting safety might be necessary before new employees can get started on their jobs. Relate the training to what they saw during your tour.

On the first day, give the trainees a safety handbook or a binder of basic safety information, rules, and policies. If you've issued them PPE, make sure they have a place to keep it. Set up a schedule for their next training sessions. Avoid information overload, but make sure they are adequately prepared for their jobs.

QUESTION: How long do I have to retain records of employee training?

ANSWER: Training requirements vary from regulation to regulation. In some cases, OSHA sets a record retention time or specifies requirements for the contents of training records, but this is not always the case. When training records are required, it would be best to always have them available.

A good practice would be to keep all training records during the worker's full period of employment. Even if a rule does not specifically require a record retention time, your company may want to set a policy to retain training records for a period after employment has been terminated. When written training records are not required, your company may still want to prepare them as a way to help keep your safety training program organized.

Here are some examples of OSHA training record requirements:

- **Asbestos (1910.1001)** — Employers are to maintain training records for one year beyond an employee's last date of employment.
- **Bloodborne pathogens (1910.1030)** — Training records must include dates of training, contents of training sessions, names and qualifications of trainers, and names and job titles of those trained. Records must be retained for three years.
- **Hazard communication (1910.1200)** — requires retraining as new hazards are introduced, but no specific written training record is required.
- **Hazardous waste operations and emergency response (HAZWOPER) (1910.120) Under the emergency response requirements at 1910.120(q),** employers must maintain a statement of training or competency. Under the requirements for hazardous waste site employees

(1910.120(e)) and treatment, storage, and disposal facilities (1910.120(p)), a written training certificate must be given to each person who has completed the training.

- **Lockout/tagout (1910.147)** — The training certification must contain each employee's name and the dates of training. OSHA does not set a record retention time.
- **Permit-required confined spaces (1910.146)** — Training certifications must include each employee's name, the signatures or initials of the trainers, and the dates of training. OSHA does not set a record retention time.
- **Personal protective equipment (1910.132)** — The training certificate must include the employee's name, the date, and the subject of the training. Employees must be able to demonstrate an understanding of the training. OSHA does not set a record retention time.
- **Powered industrial trucks (1910.178)** — The employer must certify that the operator has been trained and evaluated. The certification must include the operator's name, the dates of the training and evaluation, and the name of the trainer/evaluator. OSHA does not set a record retention time.
- **Process safety management (1910.119)** — requires retraining at least every 3 years and a written training record. No training record retention time is specified.
- **Respiratory protection (1910.134)** — no specific written training record is required. Written fit testing records must be retained until the next test takes place.

QUESTION: Is training required for respirators?

ANSWER: Yes, training must be provided to employees who are required to use respirators. The training must be comprehensive, understandable, and recur annually, and more often if necessary. This training should include at a minimum:

Why the respirator is necessary and how improper fit, use, or maintenance can compromise its protective effect.

- Limitations and capabilities of the respirator;
- Effective use in emergency situations;
- How to inspect, put on and remove, use, and check the seals;
- Maintenance and storage; and
- Recognition of medical signs and symptoms that may limit or prevent effective use.

CHAPTER 4:

WHAT TYPES OF TRAINING METHODS ARE AVAILABLE?

Most companies have matured within technology to a point where they no longer benefit from "one size fits all" training. Most training methods offer different options, such as classroom to on-line. They also offer an array of pre assessments tests that can identify skills gaps and prescribe the appropriate content. The better assessment engines and offerings, can take this type of analysis even farther, identifying skills to job tasks and competencies. This type of method can help identify skills gaps based on areas you actually need to train employees on.

Employees learn in various ways. Today, many employees are choosing on-line training as their preferred choice of training. Unfortunately, cost issues, not learning outcomes, drive many of the decisions. The most common reason organizations give for going on-line is that it's cheaper and more convenient. Each employee needs to know their learning preference relative to the method they have chosen. For example:

> Many on-line training programs require a high degree of self-motivation and discipline.

Classroom training, on the other hand, tends to be very instructor oriented leaving the employee little freedom for exploration, experimentation, and independent work. Few employees coming from the instructor-oriented classroom are well-equipped for self-motivated, self-directed, independent learning.

Most employees are used to having the instructor act as a personal trainer to help them learn. If employers really want to make training work, they need to become their own personal trainer and plan a training program that works best for them. This means paying attention to employees learning needs, figuring out how they learn best, and using this information to plan an individual path towards job success. For example:

> Some employee's may need to supplement self-paced, web-based courses with chat forums, or email support services because they know that they need to have the opportunity to ask questions and discuss training lessons.

Other employees, may need blended training to regularly use web-based training with real-world, hands-on applications in virtual classrooms with live instructor interaction because they need to practice, tape it, then watch the replay several times. With so many different types of training and so many demands on learning new skills, it is easy to become overwhelmed by all the choices, especially if an employer does not recognize how employees learn best.

Understanding the Various Training Options

To better understand how each employee learns, let's take a closer look at the choices.

> Today's learning options can be divided into two categories: Instructor led training (Classroom) and On-line (self-paced) training.

Instructor led training (ILT) is a term many employers are familiar with, and one that has taken on some new twists with the advent of the Internet. Large group classrooms are still the most popular way of attending training, and may be for quite some time. Learning from an instructor and peer in a dedicated environment with few distractions are significant benefits of this solution. Expense and time away have always been the leading drawbacks, and are becoming more so with the fast paced lifestyle most corporations have adopted.

Electronic instructor lead training (EILT) is becoming a popular alternative for employers who want most of the benefits and "feel" of being in class. The instructor can show slides, demonstrate an application, poll student responses, share and observe an application on an employee's desktop, and even assign group work.

Most services have a chat capability and share audio either through streaming it over the Internet or using a phone bridge. Some are even starting to stream video of the instructor and/or students. There are some bandwidth and technology problems surrounding all these options, but most are working through them and they won't be hurdles much longer. One of the newest features in this area is the ability to archive and "record" sessions for playback later, or during another class. This allows the employee to use this option for follow-up review or support.

Self-paced approaches have been around as long as the classroom, and, like classroom training have been enhanced with the advent of certain technologies. The biggest benefit to this category is the "anytime, anywhere" nature of the training. Methods such as books and videos have been around for a long time. Books are probably the most portable source of information ever introduced.

They often contain more information then needed making them great references for on-going support and help. Video and audiotapes work nicely for those who don't like to read great amounts of information and prefer other forms of visual or auditory engagement. Although not as portable as a book, they still free the employee from many of the limitations associated with taking a live class.

Audiotapes and videotapes should be combined in one

solution. These systems typically come on a CD-Rom and, because what this technology offers, can be a highly customized solution. The biggest drawback to all these versions of self-paced instruction is the degree of self-discipline and time needed to complete them. Also, because of the static nature of these mediums, and the rate at which technology is changing, many of these options become outdated quickly, some even as they are being released.

Training Delivery Methods

There are four types of training:

- On-the-job training
- Classroom training
- On-line training and
- Blended training

Company training programs often utilize the components of these delivery methods and formats alone or in various combinations. The training delivery methods are discussed below:

On-the-Job-Training

On-the-Job-Training (OJT) is job-related training provided by an employer in the employers' workplace. This type of training program has been designed to increase the specific job related skills of employees by providing them with related work experience specific to a specific job. Employees are trained to perform or participate in a live simulation or activity. The costs typically include the trainer's time and expenses, scheduling training sessions, and the expense of training employees.

Advantages: OSHA likes this type of training because they believe employees retain high levels of competency from a live instructor.

Disadvantages: On-the-job training is difficult to schedule when employees are spread out over several locations and it is also expensive and time-consuming to implement.

Classroom Training

Instructor-led training (ILT) methods typically feature a certified instructor who addresses a group of employees over several hours of classroom training. Instructor-led formats include lecture, guided discussion, workshop, role-playing, case study, and demonstration. Costs usually include the trainer's time and travel, training material development and program design. These costs can often include trainer meals and housing.

Advantages: An expert is available to answer questions while the employees are learning; a large number of people can be trained at the same time; trainees' interaction with one another can facilitate learning and program content can be modified quickly to meet employee's needs.

Disadvantages: This type of training causes problems with scheduling large number of employees to attend; it is also difficult in accommodating differences in employee's knowledge levels and skills.

On-Line Training

Internet-based training is self-paced which allows employees to access a specific subject any time, any place, 24/7/365. Access to the training material is established for single or multiple users via a password over a fixed time frame at a fixed fee. Internet training programs are most effective when they simulate an activity and verify that learning took place. Company costs to access the ready-to-use online programs, as with instructor-led training, per employee costs typically decrease with an increase in participation. Most online vendors also provide e-mail access to experts during the training period to answer any questions.

Advantages: Eliminates the costs of trainer time and travel; eliminates trainee scheduling and travel costs; programs can be reused on demand at multiple locations; the content and format are consistent and predictable; easy to document and track employee progress and completion of training; offers managers a growing array of choices for matching training programs to employee knowledge and skill levels.

You can also make it available to an employee who missed out on a classroom session or to a new employee in a location too far away to come to the classroom presentations. You could also use it to refresh what employees have learned in the classroom. If you provided a class a year ago, it might be even more productive to offer the material online this year, alternating between classroom and online to keep the material fresh.

Disadvantages: Outdated hardware equipment (graphics accelerators, and local area networks) can cause programs to malfunction; self-instruction offers limited opportunities to receive context-specific expert advice or timely response to questions.

Blended Training

Blended training is the newest type of learning in the workplace. Blended training programs are perhaps the highest impact, lowest cost way to drive major initiatives. Companies have discovered unique and powerful methodologies for selecting the "right media" to solve a given training problem.

Blended learning is the natural evolution of e-learning into an integrated program of multiple media types because different problems require different solutions (different mixes of media and delivery) and the key is to apply the right mix to a certain training problem. Therefore, to be successful an employer must select the right combination of media that will have the best possible training impact for the lowest possible cost.

One of the simplest approaches is to create content and "surround" it with human, interactive content. This approach of "surrounding" e-learning with human learning enables you to create high interest, accountability, and real assessment of the results of the e-learning program. For example:

> An employee could take a online forklift training course then go into the warehouse and have a hands-on demonstration.

To make blended training successful, you should start using all the various media options: classroom training, web-based training, webinars, CD-ROM courses, and videos to see what works best.

Advantages: Blended learning solves the problem of speed, scale, and impact. It leverages training where it's most appropriate, without forcing learning into places it does not fit.

Disadvantages: Unlike traditional education, corporate training exists primarily to improve business performance. We know that people learn in different ways, and different media applies to different people. The science of "how to teach adults through the internet" is still being developed.

Several others stipulate a portion of the training time to be a "hands-on" learning experience. More generally, however, the "how to" of training is left to the discretion of the employer.

Selection of Methods and Media

Training is most effective when it simulates the actual job

as closely as possible. The closer the simulation, the easier it is for the worker to transfer knowledge and skills to the job.

Sequencing Training Activities

Therefore, it is a good idea to arrange the objectives and training activities in a sequence that corresponds to the order in which the tasks are to be performed on the job. For example:

> If an employee is to learn the process of responding to a hazardous chemical leak or spill, a skill activity, the proper actions should be taught in the same order.

Various training approaches, in order of descending effectiveness, are as follows:

- The real thing (for example, handling a real label or personal protective equipment);

- A simulation (for example, practicing the handling of chemical spills using water or other harmless agents);

- Audiovisual representation (for example, a videotape showing a chemical spill being handled);

- Visuals (such as pictures of appropriate personal protective equipment);

- Lectures; and

- Handouts.

Handouts appear at the bottom of the list because there is no certainty that they will be studied or even opened when they are the only training approach. As supplements, however, handouts can be very valuable for purposes of reference and reminder. These can be useful tools for all safety training.

Methods and Media Options

Selection of methods depends on the skills and/or knowledge that you are seeking as learning outcomes. Tasks that require group interaction or team response on the job require group-oriented learning activities such as team practice, role playing or small group problem-solving sessions. Tasks that require the individual acquisition of knowledge, such as learning to understand labels or MSDS sheets can be taught to the group or by self-paced instruction, such as that provided by computer-assisted instruction.

Whatever the method of instruction, the learning activities should be developed in such a way that the employees can clearly demonstrate that they have acquired the desired skills or knowledge. Within the constraints of available resources, selection of methods and media can include the use of:

- Lectures and discussions;

- Small group practice exercises;

- Individualized instruction via computer or hard copy;

- Charts and diagrams;

- Manuals, containing a summary of the material and a glossary or reference materials;

- Slides, either purchased or taken at your facility;

- Overhead transparencies, which can be prepared ahead of time or used as blank areas to record examples and suggestions from the group;

- PowerPoint slides, which can be used in the same way;

- Videos, either purchased or home-made, to supplement instruction;

- A chalkboard or easel pads, to list key points or to record discussion points and questions; and

- Handouts.

Each of these methods and media have their own advantages and disadvantages, and are appropriate for different purposes. A survey of chemical manufacturers found that audiovisual aids such as videos and overhead transparencies, and on-the-job training were most commonly used, but the audiovisual aids were most probably accompanied by some type of lecture.

Small companies usually cannot afford sophisticated training aids, and the "trainer" is someone who wears many hats. However, many small companies have managed to conduct effective training by using several different strategies. These include:

- Piggybacking segments of training on regularly scheduled safety meetings;

- Selecting one or more employees, usually supervisors, to be the "trainers", and making them responsible for the training after attending a "train-the-trainer" course;

- Developing home-made training aids, using slides or videos, to depict actual scenes of employees in the workplace;

- Sending employees off-site to locally offered courses for training in the general elements;

- Combining training with other courses required by regulations. For example, some basic elements of the OSHA Hazwoper standard overlap with hazard communication, and it is possible to satisfy parts of both requirements at the same time. This also is helpful to the employees, since both refer to the same chemical hazards; and

- Using free or low cost training materials made available through trade associations, unions, OSHA, and other sources.

These ideas have, in many cases, resulted in training programs that are equally as good as, and sometimes more effective than, expensive programs. A brief summary of the pros and cons of common methods and media follows:

Methods and Media - Pros and Cons

Method	Pros	Cons
Lecture	Can cover lots of information Used with large and small groups Total control of information by lecturer	Doesn't encourage participation One-way communication limits understanding of learner needs Inappropriate for teaching skills No way of measuring whether learners comprehend
Discussion	Involves learners actively Instructor gets valuable feedback on learner needs Learners can discover new concepts Learning climate is more relaxed	Can go off on tangents Requires skill in maintaining class control Open-ended questions must be carefully structured for discovery to occur
Demos	Relates information to the real world Attention-getting. Can be geared to learners' capabilities Excellent for skills training when accompanied by learner practice	Requires thorough preparation Should be limited to small groups or one-on-one (Closed circuit TV can be used for some demonstrations)

Methods and Media - Pros and Cons (continued)

Method	Pros	Cons
Small Group Activities	Can be used to break up large groups Builds group rapport Excellent opportunity to apply new knowledge Can simulate many real-world problems/situations	Practice activities must be structured in detail Dominant personalities may overwhelm less aggressive Group size may be restrictive - should be limited to 3-7 learners per small group
Independent Study, Computer Assisted Instruction, Interactive Video, Distance Learning	Learners can proceed at their own speed Learner gets feedback on level of mastery Eliminates negative peer pressure CAI can be remote, yet connected to a central source Can interact without a keyboard CD-Rom adds realistic pictures and movement Employees increasingly familiar with computers	Highly dependent on quality of media used Absence of human interaction More effective for teaching knowledge than teaching skills Hardware/software can become outdated quickly Requires extensive development time Requires computer literacy
Overhead Trans-parencies	Very versatile Easy to produce on copy machine Simple to control and operate, inexpensive	Are large; require storage arrangements Information must be brief, or will be too difficult to read

Methods and Media - Pros and Cons (continued)

Method	Pros	Cons
35mm Slides	Easily handled and stored Flexible, adaptable Can be combined with taped narration for repeatability	Loose slides easily disorganized Requires photographic skills Commercially available programs not always relevant to your operations
Power Point/ Computer Projection	Extremely versatile - all Advantages of 35mm slides Can be easily modified/adapted Can be used in conjunction with distance learning	Requires computer literacy Equipment can be expensive initially
Videos	Permits same image to be played to large numbers of people at many locations Can be shot in-house to reflect site-specific operations	Image display limited to size of monitor Equipment standards not uniform worldwide Commercially available programs not always relevant
Blackboard Chart Pad	Flexible for controlling discussion Excellent for emphasis Inexpensive	Not good for complicated topics Not good for keeping permanent records Possible loss of consistency from one group to the next

Purchased Programs

You may decide to purchase training programs to supplement your training. If so, you should ask yourself the following questions:

- Does this program meet precisely the needs I have identified?

- If not, is there some built-in flexibility that will allow me to make appropriate modifications?

- Could it be used to supplement what I already have, or for retraining?

- Are there some data I can see that indicate that this program has been effective with groups of workers similar to these?

- Is the vendor willing to give me names of previous clients, so that I can find out what they think of its effectiveness?

- Can I preview all or part of the program?

- Is there a Lesson Plan or Leader's Guide that will help me to administer the training program?

- Are there manuals or handouts for the employees that will help them to remember and apply the knowledge and/or skills?

- Are there tests or quizzes that will help me to document our employees' understanding of the content of the program?

Combining Methods and Media

Effective programs generally combine methods and media. Let's look at Joe Oshacrat. He has prioritized his training activities, and knows who has to be trained about what. He has also assessed the training task, the characteristics of his employee population, and the resources available to him. He has prepared some simple learning objectives, and now has to make some decisions about methods and media. Once his decisions are made, he writes brief notes to himself to keep himself on track with each instructional session.

His decisions are as follows:

- 20 employees are given training. Joe uses standardized Lesson Plans supplemented with overhead transparencies made on the copy machine. He plans to acquire equipment eventually that will allow him to show the same information in the form of computer-generated PowerPoint slides. He also shows a commercially available video on the Hazard Communication Standard, and distributes a pamphlet that came with the video, containing the facts about it. Joe makes notes to himself to incorporate information unique to his operation into the training session, such as the location of the inventory, MSDS sheets, and written program. He encourages discussion from the employees, and responds to their concerns. The training is conducted in several 20-minute sessions during new employee orientation.

- Employees receive the training on the chemical category "flammables." Joe uses a standardized Lesson Plan for this, but adds details pertinent to the operation. For the two chemicals with different properties, he shows the individual MSDSs as overhead transparencies for discussion purposes. He prepares a simple handout containing the objectives of the training, a summary of the information on flammables, and copies of the MSDS sheets. He includes the three maintenance people in this training session, since they are likely to encounter all hazards.

- The three maintenance people also attend this session. However, Joe then takes the opportunity to spend extra time with the three employees with maintenance duties, to make sure that they have the "big picture" of all the potential hazards in the facility.

- Joe documents all training, and realizes that he must follow up to check if employees have transferred their hazard communication knowledge and skills to the job.

Although Joe Oshacrat's approach is simple and low cost, it is just as effective as programs using more expensive methods and media. It is probably more effective than generic "one-shot" training programs that do not target site-specific needs.

Summary

A summary of the steps that lead to the selection of appropriate methods and media follows.

Summary of Methods and Media Selection

- *Define the resources:* Note any limiting conditions for both development and implementation of the training program in terms of time, costs and resources available;

- *Define the size of the group:* Decide whether you will have to conduct individual, small group or large group instruction;

- *Define population characteristics:* Note educational levels, language preferences, and other considerations;

- *Define task characteristics:* Note the types of desired learning outcomes;

- *List the learning objectives* for the types of learning that you have defined;

- *Arrange the objectives in the desired sequence* to simulate the job as closely as possible;

- *List the methods/media options* from which a choice is to be made, and check the advantages and disadvantages of each;

- *Make final methods/media choices;*

- *Write guidelines to the instructor* for presenting the unit of instruction, including notes on instructional events, such as discussion sessions, and

- *Write brief guidelines for the students* if necessary, to assist them in using the media correctly; for example for computer-assisted instruction.

PART II:

WHAT ARE THE OSHA TRAINING REQUIREMENTS?

CHAPTER 5:

WHAT ARE THE OSHA GENERAL INDUSTRY TRAINING STANDARDS?

The General Industry Training Standards

The OSHA General Industry training standards are located in 29 CFR Part 1910. There are a lot of them. There are two separate volumes in the Code of Federal Regulations which contain them all.

You don't have to read them all. Read over the titles for each subpart. All of the subpart titles are listed below. Some will obviously not be applicable to your business, so skip those. Concentrate on the ones that might be applicable. Then read the discussion of those subparts in the next few pages of this book.

Part 1910 is divided into 21 subparts, each of which is designated by a capital letter and a title. Three of them (A, B and C) do not contain any applicable substantive requirements. The remaining 18 are listed below:

- Subpart D   Walking-Working Surfaces
- Subpart E   Means of Egress
- Subpart F   Powered Platforms,Manlifts, and Vehicle-Mounted Work Platforms
- Subpart G   Occupational Health and Environmental Controls
- Subpart H   Hazardous Materials
- Subpart I   Personal Protective Equipment
- Subpart J   Environmental Controls
- Subpart K   Medical and First Aid
- Subpart L   Fire Protection
- Subpart M   Compressed Gas and

- Compressed Air Equipment
- Subpart N   Materials Handling & Storage
- Subpart O   Machinery& Machine Guarding
- Subpart P   Hand and Portable Powered Tools and Other Handheld Equipment
- Subpart Q   Welding, Cutting and Brazing
- Subpart R   Special Industries
- Subpart S   Electrical
- Subpart T   Commercial Diving Operations
- Subpart Z   Toxic and Hazardous Substances

Figure 5.1. Subpart D – Walking-Working Surfaces

Subpart D – Walking-Working Surfaces Training Requirements	
1910.25	Portable wood ladders
1910.26	Portable metal ladders
1910.27	Fixed ladders
1910.28	Safety requirements for scaffolding

There are four training requirements in Walking Working surfaces. If you have ladders or scaffolds, you will want to read those sections to see what is required and whether the requirements apply to you.

If you have employees who use ladders, then §1910.25, §1910.26 & §1910.27.

Training Applies To:

Who: This training applies to all employees who use walking working surfaces, including ladders and scaffolds.

When: Employees must be trained prior to initial exposure and when using any new equipment in the workplace. The program shall enable each employee to recognize hazards related to ladders and shall train each employee in the procedures to be followed to minimize these hazards.

The employer shall ensure that each employee has been trained by a competent person in the following areas, as applicable:

- The nature of fall hazards in the work area;

- The correct procedures for erecting, maintaining, and disassembling the fall protection systems to be used;

- The proper construction, use, placement, and care in handling of all ladders;

- The maximum intended load-carrying capacities of ladders; and

- Retraining shall be provided for each employee as necessary so that the employee maintains the understanding and knowledge.

Do employees use Scaffolds then §1910.28.

Training Applies To:

Tube and Coupler Scaffolds

Tube and coupler scaffolds shall be limited in heights and working levels to those permitted in tables D-13, 14, and 15, of this section. Drawings and specification of all tube and coupler scaffolds above the limitations in tables D-13, 14, and 15 of this section shall be designed by a registered professional engineer and copies made available to the employer and for inspection purposes.

All tube and coupler scaffolds shall be constructed and erected to support four times the maximum intended loads, or as set forth in the specifications by a registered professional engineer, copies which shall be made available to the employer and for inspection purposes.

All tube and coupler scaffolds shall be erected by competent and experienced personnel.

Tubular Welded Frame Scaffolds

Drawings and specifications for all frame scaffolds over 125 feet in height above the base plates shall be designed by a registered professional engineer and copies made available to the employer and for inspection purposes.

All tubular welded frame scaffolds shall be erected by competent and experienced personnel.

Frames and accessories for scaffolds shall be maintained in good repair and every defect, unsafe condition, or noncompliance with this section shall be immediately corrected before further use of the scaffold. Any broken, bent, excessively rusted, altered, or otherwise structurally damaged frames or accessories shall not be used.

Periodic inspections shall be made of all welded frames and accessories, and any maintenance, including painting, or minor corrections authorized by the manufacturer, shall be made before further use.

Masons' Adjustable Multiple-point Suspension Scaffolds

Each scaffold shall be installed or relocated in accordance

with designs and instructions, of a registered professional engineer, and supervised by a competent, designated person.

Stone Setters' Adjustable Multiple-point Suspension Scaffolds

Each scaffold shall be installed or relocated in accordance with designs and instructions of a registered professional engineer, and such installation or relocation shall be supervised by a competent designated person.

Figure 5.2. Subpart E – Means of Egress

Subpart E – Means of Egress Training Requirements	
1910.38	Employee emergency plans and fire prevention plans

There is only one training requirement that applies in Subpart E Means of Egress.

If in the event of an emergency your employees respond to the emergency or evacuate the building then Emergency Action Plans §1910.38.

Training Applies To:

Who: The employer must designate and train employees to assist in a safe and orderly evacuation. The employer must review the emergency action plan with each employee covered by the plan as follows.

When: The training will apply when the employee is assigned initially to a job; when the employee's responsibilities under the plan change; and when the plan is changed.

If your employees work in a building, then this applies to

you. Its purpose is to ensure that when people need to have a safe and efficient means of leaving a building under emergency circumstances, the means will be there, and that they will have minimal problems finding and using them.

Egress: "A place or means of going out."

While escaping from fires is certainly a primary reason for emergency egress from a building, it is not the only reason. Additional hazards that must be considered include:

- Explosion
- Earthquake
- Smoke (without fire)
- Toxic vapors
- Storms (tornado, hurricane, etc.)
- Flash floods
- Nuclear radiation exposure and
- Actions or threatened actions of terrorist groups, and similar persons.

Each of those hazards to the occupants of a building can occur singly or in combination with others. Depending on the hazards, the people involved, the characteristics of the building, and the quality of the means of egress provided, each hazard can be compounded by:

- Panic and confusion
- Poor visibility
- Lack of information or misinformation

These compounding factors frequently cause more injuries and fatalities than the hazard itself. Providing the proper means of egress can enable persons to successfully escape from the primary hazard.

Figure 5.3. Subpart F – Powered Platforms

Subpart F – Powered Platforms, Manlifts, and Vehicle-Mounted Work Platforms Training Requirements	
1910.66	Powered platforms for building maintenance
1910.67	Vehicle-mounted elevating and rotating work platforms
1910.68	Manlifts

The Powered Platforms standards are of rather limited application. They apply only to employers who use the particular kinds of equipment listed in its title during building maintenance operations.

If employees use Powered Platforms then §1910.66, §1910.67 & §1910.68.

Training Applies To:

Who: This training applies to all employees who operate powered platforms. Working platforms shall be operated only by persons who are proficient in the operation, safe use and inspection of the particular working platform to be operated. Before using a personal fall arrest system, and after any component or system is changed, employees shall be trained in the safe use of the system.

All employees who operate working platforms shall be trained in the following:

- Recognition of, and preventive measures for, the safety hazards associated with their individual work tasks;
- General recognition and prevention of safety hazards associated with the use of working

platforms, including the provisions relating to the particular working platform to be operated;

- Emergency action plan procedures; and
- Personal fall arrest system inspection, care, use and system performance.

When: Training of employees in the operation and inspection of working platforms shall be done by a competent person.

Written work procedures for the operation, safe use, and inspection of working platforms shall be provided for employee training. Pictorial methods of instruction, may be used in lieu of written work procedures, if employee communication is improved using this method. The operating manuals supplied by manufacturers for platform systems components can serve as the basis for these procedures.

The employer shall certify that employees have been trained in operating and inspecting a working platform by preparing a certification record which includes the identity of the person trained, the signature of the person trained, the signature of the employer or the person who conducted the training and the date the training was completed.

The certification record shall be prepared at the completion of the training and shall be maintained in a file for the duration of the employee's employment. The certification record shall be kept readily available for review by the Assistant Secretary of Labor or the Assistant Secretary's representative.

Vehicle-mounted Elevating/Rotating Work Platforms

Lift controls shall be tested each day prior to use to determine that such controls are in safe working condition. Only trained persons shall operate an aerial lift.

Belting off to an adjacent pole, structure, or equipment while working from an aerial lift shall not be permitted. Employees shall always stand firmly on the floor of the basket, and shall not sit or climb on the edge of the basket or use planks, ladders, or other devices for a work position.

A body belt shall be worn and a lanyard attached to the boom or basket when working from an aerial lift. Boom and basket load limits specified by the manufacturer shall not be exceeded.

The brakes shall be set and outriggers, when used, shall be positioned on pads or a solid surface. Wheel chocks shall be installed before using an aerial lift on an incline.

Manlifts

This applies to the construction, maintenance, inspection, and operation of manlifts in relation to accident hazards. Manlifts consist of platforms or brackets and accompanying handholds mounted on, or attached to an endless belt, operating vertically in one direction only and being supported by, and driven through pulleys, at the top and bottom. Manlifts are intended for conveyance of persons only. This applies to manlifts used to carry only personnel trained and authorized by the employer in their use.

All manlifts shall be inspected by a competent designated person at intervals of not more than 30 days. Limit switches shall be checked weekly. Manlifts found to be unsafe shall not be operated until properly repaired.

This periodic inspection shall cover the following items:

- Steps
- Step Fastenings
- Rails
- Rail Supports and Fastenings
- Rollers and Slides

- Belt and Belt Tension
- Handholds and Fastenings
- Floor Landings
- Guardrails
- Lubrication
- Limit Switches
- Warning Signs and Lights
- Illumination
- Drive Pulley
- Bottom (boot) Pulley and Clearance
- Pulley Supports
- Motor
- Driving Mechanism
- Brake
- Electrical Switches
- Vibration and Misalignment and
- "Skip" on up or down run when mounting step (indicating worn gears).

Figure 5.4. Subpart G – Health and Environmental Controls

Subpart G – Health and Environmental Controls Training Requirements	
1910.95	Occupational noise exposure

There is only one training requirement in Subpart G. The noise standard, §1910.95 establishes a 90 decibel limit on employee noise exposure when averaged over an eight-hour workday, and requires various protective measures at and above the 85 decibel level. If you have employees working where the noise is at or above those limits, you should provide a training program.

If employees are exposed to high levels of noise then §1910.95.

Training Applies To:

Who: The employer shall provide training in the use and care of all hearing protectors provided to employees. The employer shall institute a training program for all employees who are exposed to noise at or above an 8-hour time-weighted average of 85 decibels, and shall ensure employee participation in such program.

Where noise is known or suspected to be excessive, it is important to take readings of noise levels. When occupational noise levels are too high, every effort should be made to eliminate the problem through engineering controls.

If engineering or other administrative controls can reduce the noise levels to below the permissible noise exposure levels a Hearing Conservation Program is not required. If noise levels cannot be brought down to acceptable levels, then a training program must be implemented to comply with OSHA requirements.

When: The training program shall be repeated annually for each employee included in the hearing conservation program. Information provided in the training program shall be updated to be consistent with changes in protective equipment and work processes.

The employer shall ensure that each employee is informed of the following:

- The effects of noise on hearing;
- The purpose of hearing protectors, the advantages, disadvantages, and attenuation of various types, and instructions on selection, fitting, use, and care; and
- The purpose of audiometric testing, and an explanation of the test procedures.

Figure 5.5. Subpart H – Hazardous Materials

Subpart H – Hazardous Materials Training Requirements	
1910.106	Flammable and combustible liquids
1910.109	Explosives and blasting agents
1910.110	Storage and handling of liquefied petroleum gases
1910.111	Storage and handling of anhydrous ammonia
1910.119	Process safety management of highly hazardous chemicals
1910.120	Hazardous waste operations and emergency response

Subpart H includes six standards that have training requirements. If you use any of the following substances or processes in your business, you should familiarize yourself with the relevant OSHA standards.

OSHA standard §1910.106 applies to the handling, storage, and use of flammable and combustible liquids with a flash point below 200°F.

There are two primary hazards associated with those flammable and combustible liquids: explosion and fire. In order to prevent those hazards, the standard addresses the primary concerns of design and construction, ventilation, ignition sources, and storage.

If there are liquids of that kind in your business or your facility has or uses Flammable and Combustible Liquids then §1910.106.

Training Applies To:

Who: The training program applies to all storage tank operators. Detailed printed instructions of what to do in flood emergencies are properly posted and that station operators and other employees depended upon to carry out such instructions are thoroughly informed as to the location and operation of such valves and other equipment necessary to effect these requirements.

When: Employees must be trained prior to using any explosives before operations.

If your facility has or uses Explosives and Blasting Agents, then §1910.109.

Training Applies To:

Who: The training applies to all motor vehicles transporting explosives shall only be driven by and be in charge of a driver who is familiar with the traffic regulations, and State laws.

Every motor vehicle transporting any quantity of Class A or Class B explosives shall, at all times, be attended by a driver or other attendant of the motor carrier. This attendant shall have been made aware of the class of the explosive material in the vehicle and of its inherent dangers, and shall have been instructed in the measures and procedures to be followed in order to protect the public from those dangers.

When: The employee shall be made familiar with the vehicle assigned, and shall be trained, supplied with the necessary means, and authorized to move the vehicle when required.

The operator shall be trained in the safe operation of the vehicle together with its mixing, conveying, and related equipment; the employer shall assure that the operator is familiar with the commodities being delivered and the general procedure for handling emergency situations.

Vehicles transporting blasting agents shall only be driven by and be in charge of a driver in possession of a valid motor vehicle operator's license. Such a person shall also be familiar with the States vehicle and traffic laws.

The operator shall be trained in the safe operation of the vehicle together with its mixing, conveying, and related equipment. He shall be familiar with the commodities being delivered and the general procedure for handling emergency situations.

If your facility has or uses Liquefied Petroleum Gases (LP-Gas), then §1910.110.

Training Applies To:

Who: The training applies to all personnel performing installation, removal, operation, and maintenance work shall be properly trained in all functions. When standard watch service is provided, it shall be extended to the LP-Gas installation and personnel properly trained.

When: Training shall be prior or at the time of initial assignment.

If your facility has or uses Anhydrous Ammonia, then §1910.111.

Training Applies To:

Who: The employer shall train all employees to ensure that unloading operations are performed by reliable persons properly instructed and given the authority to monitor careful compliance with all applicable procedures.

When: Training shall be prior or at the time of initial assignment.

The Process Safety Management standard §1910.119 only applies to processes that involve some 125 specific chemicals (listed by name and CAS number in Appendix A of OSHA standard §1910.119) when used in quantities exceeding specified thresholds listed in that Appendix, and processes that involve a flammable liquid or gas on site in one location in a quantity of 10,000 pounds or more.

This standard does not apply to oil or gas well drilling or servicing operations, retail facilities, or normally unoccupied remote facilities.

If employees are involved in unexpected releases of toxic, reactive, or flammable liquids and gases in processes involving Highly Hazardous Chemicals then Process Safety Management §1910.119.

Training Applies To:

Who: Each employee presently involved in operating a process, and each employee before being involved in operating a newly assigned process, shall be trained in an overview of the process and in the operating procedures. The training shall include emphasis on the specific safety and health hazards, emergency operations including shutdown, and safe work practices applicable to the employee's job tasks.

When: In lieu of initial training for those employees already involved in operating a process an employer may certify in writing that the employee has the required knowledge, skills, and abilities to safely carry out the duties and responsibilities as specified in the operating procedures.

Refresher training shall be provided at least every three years, and more often if necessary, to each employee involved in operating a process to assure that the employee understands and adheres to the current operating procedures of the process. The employer, in consultation with the employees involved in operating the process, shall determine the appropriate frequency of refresher training.

The employer shall ascertain that each employee involved in operating a process has received and understood the training required. The employer shall prepare a record which contains the identity of the employee, the date of training, and the means used to verify that the employee understood the training.

Contract Employer Responsibilities Training

The contract employer shall assure that each contract employee is trained in the work practices necessary to safely perform his/her job.

The contract employer shall assure that each contract employee is instructed in the known potential fire, explosion, or toxic release hazards related to his/her job and the process, and the applicable provisions of the emergency action plan.

The contract employer shall document that each contract employee has received and understood the training required by this paragraph. The contract employer shall prepare a record which contains the identity of the contract employee, the date of training, and the means used to verify that the employee understood the training.

Mechanical Integrity Training

The employer shall train each employee involved in maintaining the on-going integrity of process equipment in an overview of that process and its hazards and in the procedures applicable to the employee's job tasks to assure that the employee can perform the job tasks in a safe manner.

Management of Change Training

Employees involved in operating a process and maintenance and contract employees whose job tasks will be affected by a change in the process shall be informed of, and trained in, the change prior to start-up of the process or affected part of the process.

The final standard in Subpart H is §1910.120 Hazardous Waste Operations and Emergency Response.

The title of the OSHA standard regulating hazardous waste and emergency response, OSHA standard §1910.120, is often misunderstood. The standard is, in actuality, two separate standards. One regulates hazardous waste operations, §1910.120(a) through §1910.120(p).

The other, §1910.120(q), is designed to control spills and releases of any hazardous substance no matter where it occurs. If either of those matters is a concern in your business, familiarize yourself with the applicable provisions of that standard.

If your employees are involved with Hazardous Waste and Emergency Response Operations (Hazwoper) then §1910.120.

Training Applies To:

Who: Employees who work at a hazardous waste site and those who are managers or supervisors at a hazardous waste site require training.

Employees who work at a Treatment, Storage, and Disposal (TSD) facility require training; and

Any employees designated to participate in emergency response to hazardous substance releases require training.

When: OSHA specifies training time requirements for all of the various duties involved.

- Employees working at a hazardous waste site must be trained before they participate in field activities and annually thereafter;
- Employees working at a TSD facility must be trained upon initial assignment and annually thereafter;
- Any employees designated to participate in emergency response to hazardous substance releases must be trained prior to taking part in actual emergency operations, and must receive annual refresher training; and
- Training certification is also required for general training; certain operations conducted under RCRA; and emergency response to hazardous substance releases. Employees and supervisors that have received and successfully completed the training and field experience shall be certified by their instructor or the head instructor and trained supervisor as having completed the necessary training. A written certificate shall be given to each person certified. Any person who has not been certified or who does not meet the requirements shall be prohibited from engaging in hazardous waste operations.

General Site Workers Training

General site workers initial training (such as equipment operators, general laborers and supervisory personnel) engaged in hazardous substance removal or other activities which expose or potentially expose workers to hazardous substances and health hazards shall receive a minimum of 40 hours of instruction off the site, and a minimum of three days actual field experience under the direct supervision of a trained experienced supervisor.

Workers on site only occasionally for a specific limited task (such as, but not limited to, ground water monitoring, land surveying, or geophysical surveying) and who are unlikely to be exposed over permissible exposure limits and published exposure limits shall receive a minimum of 24 hours of instruction off the site, and the minimum of one day actual field experience under the direct supervision of a trained, experienced supervisor.

Workers regularly on site who work in areas which have been monitored and fully characterized indicating that exposures are under permissible exposure limits and published exposure limits where respirators are not necessary, and the characterization indicates that there are no health hazards or the possibility of an emergency developing, shall receive a minimum of 24 hours of instruction off the site, and the minimum of one day actual field experience under the direct supervision of a trained, experienced supervisor.

Workers with 24 hours of training and who become general site workers or who are required to wear respirators, shall have the additional 16 hours and two days of training necessary to total the training.

Management and Supervisor Training

On-site management and supervisors directly responsible for or who supervise employees engaged in hazardous waste operations shall receive 40 hours initial and three days of supervised field experience (the training may be reduced to 24 hours and one day if the only area of their responsibility is employees and at least eight additional hours of specialized training at the time of job assignment on such topics as, but no limited to, the employer's safety and health program, personal protective equipment program, spill containment program, and health hazard monitoring procedure and techniques.

Equivalent Training

Employers who can show by documentation or certification that an employee's work experience and/or training has resulted in training equivalent to that training required shall not be required to provide the initial training requirements. However, certified employees or employees with equivalent training new to a site shall receive appropriate, site specific training before site entry and have appropriate supervised field experience at the new site. Equivalent training includes any academic training or the training that existing employees might have already received from actual hazardous waste site experience.

Emergency Response Training

Employees who are engaged in responding to hazardous emergency situations at hazardous waste clean-up sites that may expose them to hazardous substances shall be trained in how to respond to expected emergencies. Employees, managers and supervisors shall receive eight hours of refresher training annually.

Training for emergency response employees shall be completed before they are called upon to perform in real emergencies. Training shall include the elements of the emergency response plan, standard operating procedures the employer has established for the job, the personal protective equipment to be worn and procedures for handling emergency incidents.

Training shall be based on the duties and function to be performed by each responder of an emergency response organization. The skill and knowledge levels required for all new responders, those hired after the effective date of this standard, shall be conveyed to them through training before they are permitted to take part in actual emergency operations on an incident. Employees who participate, or are expected to participate, in emergency response, shall be given training in accordance with the following:

First Responder Awareness Level Training

First responders at the awareness level are individuals who are likely to witness or discover a hazardous substance release and who have been trained to initiate an emergency response sequence by notifying the proper authorities of the release. They would take no further action beyond notifying the authorities of the release. First responders at the awareness level shall have sufficient training or have had sufficient experience to objectively demonstrate competency in the following areas:

- An understanding of what hazardous substances are, and the risks associated with them in an incident;

- An understanding of the potential outcomes associated with an emergency created when hazardous substances are present;

- The ability to recognize the presence of hazardous substances in an emergency; and

- The ability to identify the hazardous substances, if possible.

First Responder Operations Level Training

First responders at the operations level are individuals who respond to releases or potential releases of hazardous substances as part of the initial response to the site for the purpose of protecting nearby persons, property, or the environment from the effects of the release. They are trained to respond in a defensive fashion without actually trying to stop the release.

Their function is to contain the release from a safe distance, keep it from spreading, and prevent exposures. First responders at the operational level shall have received at least eight hours of training or have had sufficient experience to objectively demonstrate competency in the following areas in addition to those listed for the awareness level and the employer shall certify:

- Knowledge of the basic hazard and risk assessment techniques;

- Know how to select and use proper personal protective equipment provided to the first responder operational level;

- An understanding of basic hazardous materials terms;

- Know how to perform basic control, containment and/or confinement operations within the capabilities of the resources and personal protective equipment available with their unit;

- Know how to implement basic decontamination procedures; and

- An understanding of the relevant standard operating procedures and termination procedures.

Hazardous Materials Technician Training

Hazardous materials technicians are individuals who respond to releases or potential releases for the purpose of stopping the release. They assume a more aggressive role than a first responder at the operations level in that they will approach the point of release in order to plug, patch or otherwise stop the release of a hazardous substance.

Hazardous materials technicians shall have received at least 24 hours of training equal to the first responder operations level and in addition have competency in the following areas and the employer shall certify:

- Know how to implement the employer's emergency response plan;

- Know the classification, identification and verification of known and unknown materials by using field survey instruments and equipment;

- Be able to function within an assigned role in the Incident Command System;

- Know how to select and use proper specialized chemical personal protective equipment provided to the hazardous materials technician;

- Understand hazard and risk assessment techniques;

- Be able to perform advance control, containment, and/or confinement operations within the capabilities of the resources and personal protective equipment available with the unit;

- Understand and implement decontamination procedures;

- Understand termination procedures and

- Understand basic chemical and toxicological terminology and behavior.

Hazardous Materials Specialist Training

Hazardous materials specialists are individuals who respond with and provide support to hazardous materials technicians. Their duties parallel those of the hazardous materials technician, however, those duties require a more directed or specific knowledge of the various substances they may be called upon to contain. The hazardous materials specialist would also act as the site liaison with Federal, state, local and other government authorities in regards to site activities. Hazardous materials specialists shall have received at least 24 hours of training equal to the technician level and in addition have competency in the following areas and the employer shall certify:

- Know how to implement the local emergency response plan;

- Understand classification, identification and verification of known and unknown materials by using advanced survey instruments and equipment;

- Know the state emergency response plan;

- Be able to select and use proper specialized chemical personal protective equipment provided to the hazardous materials specialist;

- Understand in-depth hazard and risk techniques;

- Be able to perform specialized control, containment, and/or confinement operations within the capabilities of the resources and personal protective equipment available;

- Be able to determine and implement decontamination procedures;

- Have the ability to develop a site safety and control plan; and

- Understand chemical, radiological and toxicological terminology and behavior.

On Scene Incident Commander Training

Incident commanders, who will assume control of the incident scene beyond the first responder awareness level, shall receive at least 24 hours of training equal to the first responder operations level and in addition have competency in the following areas and the employer shall so certify:

- Know and be able to implement the employer's incident command system;

- Know how to implement the employer's emergency response plan;

- Know and understand the hazards and risks associated with employees working in chemical protective clothing;

- Know how to implement the local emergency response plan;

- Know of the state emergency response plan and of the Federal Regional Response Team; and

- Know and understand the importance of decontamination procedures.

Post-Emergency Response Training

Where the clean-up is done on plant property using plant or workplace employees, employees shall have completed the training requirements of the following: Emergency action plans (§1910.38), Respiratory protection (§1910.134) and Hazard Communication (§1910.1200) and other appropriate safety and health training made necessary by the tasks they are expected to perform such as personal protective equipment and decontamination procedures.

Refresher Training

Those employees who are trained shall receive annual refresher training of sufficient content and duration to maintain their competencies, or shall demonstrate competency in those areas at least yearly.

A statement shall be made of the training or competency, and if a statement of competency is made, the employer shall keep a record of the method used to demonstrate competency.

Figure 5.6. Subpart I – Personal Protective Equipment

Subpart I – Personal Protective Equipment Training Requirements	
1910.132	General requirements
1910.133	Eye and face protection
1910.134	Respiratory protection
1910.135	Head protection
1910.136	Foot protection
1910.138	Hand protection

Personal protective equipment (PPE) standards include those containing general training requirements for all PPE §1910.132 - §1910.138 standards that meet design, selection, and use requirements for specific types of PPE (eye, face, head, foot, and hand).

They contain training requirements covering equipment selection, defective and damaged equipment, training, and hazards to the hands.

The Personal Protective Equipment standards §1910.132 through §1910.138 establish the employer's obligation to provide PPE to employees. The standard also requires employers to pay for PPE required by the company for the worker to do his/her job safely in compliance with OSHA standards.

The PPE standard has been interpreted to cover everything that could conceivably be regarded as "personal protective equipment" and every situation that could even remotely be deemed "hazardous."

§1910.133 covers eye and face protection and requires that each affected employee use appropriate eye or face protection when exposed to eye or face hazards from flying particles, molten metal, liquid chemicals, acids or caustic fluids, chemical gases or vapors, or potentially injurious light radiation.

If you have a respirator or gas mask on your premises, even if no one ever uses it, you must comply with the Respiratory Protection standard §1910.134. It requires, among other things, that you establish and maintain a respiratory protection program. That means you must have it in a written program.

§1910.135 covers head protection and requires each affected employee to wear protective helmets when working in areas where there is potential for injury to the head from falling objects. Protective helmets must also be designed to reduce electrical shock hazards when employees are working near exposed electrical conductors.

§1910.136 covers foot protection and requires each affected employee to wear protective footwear when working in areas where there is a danger of foot injuries due to falling and rolling objects, objects piercing the sole, and where an employee's feet are exposed to electrical hazards.

Safety shoes or boots will provide employees both impact and compression protection. Where necessary, safety shoes can be obtained which provide puncture protection. Safety footwear is required for employees who regularly handle solid objects weighing 15 pounds or more that can fall on their toes. For protection of feet and legs from falling or rolling objects, sharp objects, molten metal, hot surfaces, and wet slippery surfaces, workers should use appropriate foot-guards, safety shoes or boots and leggings.

Employees that work around exposed electrical wires will need to wear metal-free non-conductive shoes or boots. Rubber or synthetic footwear is recommended when working around chemicals. Avoid wearing leather shoes or boots when working because these substances can eat through the leather right to your foot. Safety shoes or boots with impact protection will be required for carrying or handling materials such as packages, objects, parts or heavy tools, which could be dropped; and, for other activities where objects might fall onto the feet.

§1910.138 covers hand protection and requires employees to use appropriate hand protection when employee's hands are exposed to hazards such as those from skin absorption of harmful substances; severe cuts or lacerations; severe abrasions; punctures; chemical burns; thermal burns; and harmful temperature extremes.

If employees use Personal Protective Equipment then OSHA standards 1910.132 - 1910.138.

Training Applies To:

Who: This training applies to all employees who use Personal Protective Equipment. This includes shoes, gloves, glasses, and hard hats.

When: The employer shall provide training to each employee who is required to use PPE. Each employee shall be trained to know at least the following:

- When PPE is necessary;
- What PPE is necessary;
- How to properly don, doff, adjust and wear PPE;
- The limitations of the PPE; and,
- The proper care, maintenance, useful life, and disposal of the PPE.

Each affected employee shall demonstrate an understanding of the training given and the ability to use PPE properly before being allowed to perform work requiring the use of PPE.

When the employer has reason to believe that any affected employee who has already been trained does not have the understanding and skill required the employer shall retrain each such employee. Circumstances where retraining is required include, but are not limited to, situations where:

- Changes in the workplace render previous training obsolete, or
- Changes in the types of PPE to be used render previous training obsolete; or
- Inadequacies in an affected employee's knowledge or use of assigned PPE indicate that the employee has not retained the requisite understanding or skill.

The employer shall verify that each affected employee has received and understood the required training through a written certification that contains the name of each employee trained, the date(s) of training, and that identifies the subject of the certification.

Figure 5.8. Subpart J – General Environmental Controls

Subpart J – General Environmental Controls Training Requirements	
1910.145	Accident prevention signs and tags
1910.146	Permit-required confined spaces
1910.147	Control of hazardous energy (lockout/tagout)

Subpart J contains three training requirements.

§1910.145 covers the specifications for accident prevention signs and tags, that are to be used on safety cans, emergency stop bars on machines, and physical hazards that can result in an employee tripping, falling, stumbling, striking against or being caught in-between.

If employers use Accident Prevention Signs and Tags to warn or give instructions then §1910.145.

Training Applies To:

Who: This training applies to all employees who are exposed to sign and tags to communicate safety hazards. Hazards exist in every workplace, and employers have a responsibility to train their employees. One of the easiest ways to accomplish this is with accident prevention signs. These specifications apply to the design, application and use of signs or symbols used to prevent accidental injuries or property damage. Tags can also be used to warn employees who are exposed to hazardous conditions.

When: There is no specific training time mentioned in the OSHA standard.

OSHA standard §1910.146 apply to each place of employment where there is a confined space. That term is defined as a space that is large enough and configured that an employee can bodily enter and perform assigned work. It has the following characteristics:

- Has limited or restricted means for entry or exit (for example, tanks, vessels, silos, storage bins, hoppers, vaults, and pits are spaces that may have limited means of entry); and

- Is not designed for continuous employee occupancy.

Is there limited or restricted means for entry or exit to the workspace then Permit-Required Confined Spaces §1910.146.

Training Applies To:

Who: This training applies to all employees who enter spaces that have limited or restricted means for or exit. A Confined space training program will help all employees whose work involves confined spaces. It will help them acquire the understanding, knowledge and skills necessary for the safe performance of their assigned duties.

When: Training will be provided to each affected employee as follows:

- Before the employee is first assigned duties that involved confined spaces;
- Before there is a change in assigned duties;
- Whenever there is a change in permit space operations that presents a hazard which an employee has not previously been trained; and
- Whenever there is any reason to believe either that there are deviations from the confined space entry procedures required by the OSHA standard or that

there are inadequacies in the employee's knowledge or use of those procedures.

The training must be conducted in a manner that will establish employee proficiency in the duties required by the OSHA standard. It will also introduce new or revised procedures, as necessary, in order to accomplish full compliance.

Upon its completion, a written certification shall be executed that the training required by the OSHA standard has been accomplished. The certification shall contain each employee's name, the signatures or initials of the trainers, and the dates of training. The certification will be available for inspection by employees and their authorized representatives.

If there are machines in your business that are ever repaired, serviced or maintained, and could cause the unexpected start up or release of Stored Energy then Lockout/ Tagout §1910. 147.

Training Applies To:

Who: The training applies to all employees who perform services or maintenance equipment that must be locked out or tagged out. The employer must provide training to ensure that the purpose and function of the program are understood by employees, and that they acquire the knowledge and skills required for the safe application, use and removal of the energy controls.

When: The training must include the following:

- Each authorized employee must receive training in the recognition of applicable hazardous energy sources, the type and magnitude of the energy available in the workplace, and the methods and means necessary for energy isolation and control;

- Each affected employee must be instructed in the purpose and use of the energy control procedure;
- All other employees must be instructed about the procedure, and about the prohibition on restarting or reenergizing machines or equipment which are locked out or tagged out, if their work operations are or may be in an area where energy control procedures may be utilized; and
- All new employees must be trained.

Additional Training

When tagout systems are used, employees must also be trained in the following limitations of tags:

- Tags are essentially warning devices affixed to energy isolating devices; they do not provide the physical restraint provided by a lock;
- When a tag is attached, it is not to be removed without authorization of the authorized person responsible; it is never to be bypassed, ignored or otherwise defeated;
- In order to be effective, tags must be legible and understandable by all employees;
- Tags and their means of attachment must be made of materials which will withstand the environmental conditions encountered in the workplace;
- Tags may evoke a false sense of security. They are only one part of an overall energy control program; and
- Tags must be securely attached to energy isolating devices so that they cannot be inadvertently or accidentally detached during use.

Employee Retraining

Retraining must be provided for all authorized and affected employees whenever there is a change in their job assignments, a change in machines, equipment or processes that present a new hazard, or when there is a change in energy control procedures.

Additional retraining must also be conducted whenever a periodic inspection reveals the employer has reason to believe that there are inadequacies in the employee's knowledge or use of the energy control procedures. The retraining must reestablish employee proficiency and introduce new or revised control methods and procedures.

The employer must certify that employee training has been accomplished and is being kept up to date; certification must contain each employee's name and dates of training. All authorized or affected employers should be retrained at least annually.

Figure 5.9. Subpart K – Medical and First Aid

Subpart K – Medical and First Aid Training Requirements	
1910.151	Medical services and first aid

Subpart K is one of the briefest of all general industry training subparts. It requires that you have a person with first aid training on hand unless there is a hospital, clinic or infirmary "in near proximity," ensure the "ready availability" of medical personnel, and have "suitable facilities" for quick drenching or flushing of the eyes and body whenever your employees could be exposed to "injurious corrosive materials."

If you do not have arrangements with a medical clinic in near proximity to your plant for the treatment of employees then Medical Services and First Aid §1910.151.

Training Applies To:

Who: This training applies to all designated first-aid providers when there is no infirmary, clinic or hospital in near proximity to the workplace which is used for the treatment of all injured employees. A person or persons must be adequately trained to render first aid.

First aid supplies approved by the consulting physician must be readily available. Where the eyes or body of any person may be exposed to injurious corrosive materials, suitable facilities for quick drenching or flushing of the eyes and body must be provided within the work area for immediate emergency use.

When: An employee must be trained prior to providing first aid in emergency situations.

Figure 5.10. Subpart L – Fire Protection

Subpart L –Fire Protection Training Requirements	
1910.156	Fire brigades
PORTABLE FIRE SUPPRESSION EQUIPMENT	
1910.157	Portable fire extinguishers
1910.158	Standpipe and hose systems
FIXED FIRE SUPPRESSION EQUIPMENT	
1910.160	Fixed extinguishing systems, general
FIRE PROTECTION SYSTEMS	
1910.164	Fire detection systems
1910.165	Employee alarm systems

Subpart L contains various training requirements for fire protection systems and equipment including fire brigades, and portable and fixed fire suppression equipment, fire detection systems, and fire and employee alarm systems that are installed in order to meet the OSHA's fire protection requirements.

Fire brigade §1910.156 does not require an employer to organize a fire brigade but, if he or she chooses to do so, it imposes numerous requirements that must be observed.

If employees use fire-fighting equipment then Fire Brigades §1910.156.

Training Applies To:

Who: This training applies to all employees who use fire-fighting equipment in their facility; this includes fire brigades, portable fire extinguishers, hose and stand pipe system, fire detection systems, and fire alarm systems.

When: The employer shall assure that training and education is conducted frequently enough to assure that each member of the fire brigade is able to perform the member's assigned duties and functions satisfactorily and in a safe manner so as not to endanger fire brigade members or others employees. All fire brigade members shall be provided with training at least annually. In addition, fire brigade members who are expected to perform interior structural fire fighting shall be provided with an education session or training at least quarterly.

The employer shall prepare and maintain a statement or written policy which establishes the existence of a fire brigade; the basic organizational structure; the type, amount, and frequency of training to be provided to fire brigade members; the expected number of members in the fire brigade; and the functions that the fire brigade is to perform at the workplace.

The employer shall provide training and education for all fire brigade members commensurate with those duties and functions that fire brigade members are expected to perform. Such training and education shall be provided to fire brigade members before they perform fire brigade emergency activities. Fire brigade leaders and training instructors shall be provided with training and education which is more comprehensive than that provided to the general membership of the fire brigade.

The employer shall inform fire brigade members about special hazards such as storage and use of flammable liquids and gases, toxic chemicals, radioactive sources, and water reactive substances, to which they may be exposed during fire and other emergencies.

The fire brigade members shall also be advised of any changes that occur in relation to the special hazards. The employer shall develop and make available for inspection by fire brigade members, written procedures that describe the actions to be taken in situations involving the special hazards and shall include these in the training and education program.

If you have portable fire extinguishers on the premises, the nature of your OSHA obligations depends upon whether or not your employees will use those extinguishers to fight fires.

Do employees use Portable Fire Extinguishers then OSHA standard §1910.157.

Training Applies To:

Who: This training applies to all employers that have provided portable fire extinguishers for employee use in the workplace, he or she must also provide an educational program to familiarize employees with the general principles of fire extinguisher use and the hazards involved with fighting incipient fires.

When: The employer must provide this education upon initial employment and at least annually thereafter.

If an employer has developed an emergency action plan, then only those employees designated to use fire fighting equipment need to be trained in the use of the appropriate equipment. This training is required upon initial assignment to this designated group of employees and at least annually thereafter.

Do employees use Standpipe and Hose Systems then OSHA standard §1910.158.

Training Applies To:

The employer shall assure that standpipes are located or otherwise protected against mechanical damage. Damaged standpipes shall be repaired promptly.

Who: The employer shall designate trained persons to conduct all inspections required under this standard.

When: No specific training time is mentioned in the OSHA standard.

Do employees use Fixed Extinguishing Systems then OSHA standard §1910.160.

Training Applies To:

Who: The employer shall train employees designated to inspect, maintain, operate, or repair fixed extinguishing systems and annually review their training to keep them up- to-date in the functions they are to perform.

When: No specific training time is mentioned in the OSHA standard.

Do employees use Fire Detection Systems then OSHA standard §1910.164.

Training Applies To:

Who: The employer shall assure that the servicing, maintenance and testing of fire detection systems, including cleaning and necessary sensitivity adjustments, are performed by a trained person knowledgeable in the operations and functions of the system.

When: No specific training time is mentioned in the OSHA standard.

Do employees use Fire Alarm Systems then OSHA standard §1910.165.

Training Applies To:

Who: The employer shall assure that the servicing, maintenance and testing of employee alarms are done by persons trained in the designed operation and functions necessary for reliable and safe operation of the system.

When: No specific training time is mentioned in the OSHA standard.

Figure 5.12. Subpart N – Materials Handling and Storage

Subpart N – Materials Handling and Storage Training Requirements	
1910.177	Servicing multi-piece and single piece rim wheel
1910.178	Powered industrial trucks
1910.179	Overhead and gantry cranes
1910.180	Crawler locomotive and truck cranes
1910.181	Derricks
1910.183	Helicopters

Subpart N covers the moving and storage of materials, the servicing of rim wheels used on large vehicles (trucks, tractors, buses, etc.), and the use of the particular items of equipment.

§1910.177 requires training for all tire servicing employees that work on trucks, tractors, trailers, buses and off-road vehicles. It requires the utilization of industry-accepted procedures that minimize the potential for employee injury, the use of proper equipment such as clip-on chucks, restraining devices or barriers to retain the wheel components in the event of an incident during the inflation of tires, and the use of compatible components. The standard does not apply to the servicing of rim wheels used on automobiles, or on pickup trucks and vans that utilize automobile or truck tires designated "LT."

If employees Service Multi-Piece or Single-Piece Rim Wheels then §1910.177.

Training Applies To:

Who: The employer shall provide a training program to train all employees who service rim wheels in the hazards involved in servicing those rim wheels and the safety procedures to be followed.

The employer shall assume that no employee services any rim wheel unless the employee has been trained and instructed in correct procedures of servicing the rim type being serviced, and in the safe operating procedures described below:

- Information to be used in the training program shall include at a minimum, the applicable data contained in the charts, rim manuals, and the contents of this standard; and
- Where an employer knows or has reason to believe that any of his employees is unable to read and understand the charts or rim manual, the employer shall assure that the employee is instructed concerning the contents of the charts and rim manual in a manner which the employee is able to understand.

The employer shall assure that each employee demonstrates and maintains the ability to service multi-piece rim wheels safely, including performance of the following tasks:

- Demounting of tires (including deflation);
- Inspection and identification of rim wheel components;
- Mounting of tires (including inflation within a restraining device or other safeguard required by this section);
- Use of the restraining device or barrier, and other equipment required by this section;
- Handling of rim wheels;
- Inflation of tire when a single piece trim wheel is mounted on vehicle; and
- An understanding of the necessity of standing outside the trajectory both during the inflation if the tire and during inspection of the rim wheel inflation; and
- Installation and removal of rim wheels.

When: The employer shall evaluate each employee's ability to perform these tasks and to service rim wheels safely and shall provide additional training as necessary to assure that each employee maintains his or her proficiency.

Safe Operating Procedures- for Multi-piece-rim Wheels

The employer shall establish a safe operating procedure for servicing multi-piece rim wheels and shall assure that employees are instructed in and follow that procedure. The procedure shall include at least the following elements:

- Tires shall be completely deflated by removal of the valve core before demounting;
- Mounting and demounting of the tire shall be done only from the narrow ledge side of the wheel. Care

shall be taken to avoid damaging the tire beads while mounting tires on wheels. Tires shall be mounted only on compatible wheels of matching bead diameter and width;

- Nonflammable rubber lubricant shall be applied to bead and wheel mating surfaces before assembly of the rim wheel, unless the tire or wheel manufacturer recommends against the use of any rubber lubricant;
- If a tire changing machine is used, the tire shall be inflated only to the minimum pressure necessary to force the tire bead onto the rim ledge while on the tire changing machine;
- If a bead expander is used, it shall be removed before the valve core is installed and as soon as the rim wheel becomes airtight (the tire bead slips onto the bead seat);
- Tires may be inflated only when contained within a restraining device, positioned behind a barrier or bolted on the vehicle with the lug nuts fully tightened;
- Tires shall not be inflated when any flat, solid surface is in the trajectory and within one foot of the sidewall;
- Employees shall stay out of the trajectory when inflating a tire;
- Tires shall not be inflated to more than the inflation pressure stamped in the sidewall unless a higher pressure is recommended by the manufacturer;
- Tires shall not be inflated above the maximum pressure recommended by the manufacturer to seat the tire bead firmly against the rim flange;
- No heat shall be applied to a single piece wheel; and
- Cracked, broken, bent, or otherwise damaged wheels shall not be reworked, welded, brazed, or otherwise heated.

OSHA standard §1910.178 contains training requirements for Powered Industrial trucks (forklift trucks) and various requirements for fire protection, design, maintenance, and use of fork lift trucks, tractors, platform lift trucks, motorized hand trucks, and other specialized industrial trucks that are powered by electric motors or internal combustion engines.

These training requirements do not apply to compressed air or nonflammable compressed gas-operated industrial trucks, or to farm vehicles, or to vehicles intended primarily for earth moving or over-the-road hauling.

If you have employees who operate Powered Industrial Trucks (forklift trucks) then §1910.178.

Training Applies To:

Who: This training applies to all employees who operate a powered industrial truck safely, as demonstrated by the successful completion of the training and evaluation.

When: Prior to permitting an employee to operate a powered industrial truck the employer shall ensure that each operator has successfully completed the training.

Training shall consist of a combination of formal instruction (e.g., lecture, discussion, interactive computer learning, video tape, written material), practical training (demonstrations performed by the trainer and practical exercises performed by the trainee), and evaluation of the operator's performance in the workplace.

All operator training and evaluation shall be conducted by persons who have the knowledge, training, and experience to train powered industrial truck operators and evaluate their competence.

Powered industrial truck operators shall receive initial training in the following topics, except in topics which the employer can demonstrate are not applicable to safe operation of the truck in the employer's workplace.

Truck-related Training Topics:

- Operating instructions, warnings, and precautions for the types of truck the operator will be authorized to operate;
- Differences between the truck and the automobile;
- Truck controls and instrumentation: where they are located, what they do, and how they work;
- Engine or motor operation;
- Steering and maneuvering;
- Visibility (including restrictions due to loading);
- Fork and attachment adaptation, operation, and use limitations;
- Vehicle capacity;
- Vehicle stability;
- Any vehicle inspection and maintenance that the operator will be required to perform;
- Refueling and/or charging and recharging of batteries;
- Operating limitations;
- Any other operating instructions, warnings, or precautions listed in the operator's manual for the types of vehicle that the employee is being trained to operate.

Workplace-related Training Topics:

- Surface conditions where the vehicle will be operated;
- Composition of loads to be carried and load stability;
- Load manipulation, stacking, and unstacking;
- Pedestrian traffic in areas where the vehicle will be operated;
- Narrow aisles and other restricted places where the vehicle will be operated;
- Hazardous (classified) locations where the vehicle will be operated;
- Ramps and other sloped surfaces that could affect the vehicle's stability;
- Closed environments and other areas where insufficient ventilation or poor vehicle maintenance

could cause a buildup of carbon monoxide or diesel exhaust; and
- Other unique or potentially hazardous environmental conditions in the workplace that could affect safe operation.

Refresher Training

Refresher training, including an evaluation of the effectiveness of that training, shall be conducted to ensure that the operator has the knowledge and skills needed to operate the powered industrial truck safely.

Refresher training shall be provided to the operator when:

- The operator has been observed to operate the vehicle in an unsafe manner;
- The operator has been involved in an accident or near-miss incident;
- The operator has received an evaluation that reveals that the operator is not operating the truck safely;
- The operator is assigned to drive a different type of truck; or
- A condition in the workplace changes in a manner that could affect safe operation of the truck.

An evaluation of each powered industrial truck operator's performance shall be conducted at least once every three years.

Avoidance of Duplicative Training

If an operator has previously received training in a topic and the training is appropriate to the truck and working conditions encountered, then additional training in that topic is not required if the operator has been evaluated and found competent to operate the truck safely.

Certification of Training

The employer shall certify that each operator has been trained and evaluated. The certification shall include the name of the operator, the date of the training, the date of the evaluation, and the identity of the person(s) performing the training or evaluation.

OSHA standard §1910.179 applies to overhead and gantry cranes, including semi-gantry, cantilever gantry, wall cranes, storage bridge cranes, and others having the same fundamental characteristics.

If employees operate Overhead and Gantry Cranes then §1910.179.

Training Applies To:

Who: This training applies to all employees who operate Overhead and gantry cranes. Only designated personnel shall be permitted to operate a crane. When two or more cranes are used to lift a load one qualified responsible person shall be in charge of the operation. He/She shall analyze the operation and instruct all personnel involved in the proper positioning, rigging of the load, and the movements to be made.

The employer shall insure that operators are familiar with the operation and care of fire extinguishers provided

When: No specific training time is mentioned in the OSHA standard.

OSHA standard §1910.180 applies to crawler cranes, locomotive cranes, wheel-mounted cranes of both truck and self-propelled wheel type, and any variations thereof which retain the same fundamental characteristics. This standard only covers cranes of the above types, which are basically powered by internal combustion engines or electric motors and which utilize drums and ropes. Cranes designed for railway and automobile wreck clearances are excepted. The requirements of this standard are applicable only to machines when used as lifting cranes.

If employees operate Crawler Locomotive and Truck cranes then §1910.180.

Training Applies To:

Who: This training applies to all employees who operate Crawler locomotive and truck cranes. Before traveling a crane with a load, a designated person shall be responsible for determining and controlling safety. Decisions such as position of load, boom location, ground support, travel route, and speed of movement shall be in accord with his determinations.

When two or more cranes are used to lift one load, one designated person shall be responsible for the operation. He shall be required to analyze the operation and instruct all personnel involved in the proper positioning, rigging of the load, and the movements to be made.

Operating and maintenance personnel shall be made familiar with the use and care of the fire extinguishers provided.

When: Training shall be prior to or at the time of initial assignment.

The term "derrick" is defined as an apparatus consisting of a mast or equivalent member held at the head by guys or braces, with or without a boom, for use with a hoisting mechanism and operating ropes. Derricks may be permanently installed for temporary use as in construction work. This standard also applies to any modification of the types of derrick mentioned above which retain their fundamental features, except for floating derricks.

OSHA standard §1910.181 applies to guy, stiff leg, basket, breast, gin pole, Chicago boom, and A-frame derricks of the stationary type, capable of handling loads at variable reaches and powered by hoists through systems of rope reeving, used to perform lifting hook work, single or multiple line bucket work, grab, grapple, and magnet work.

If employees operate Derricks then §1910.181.

Training Applies To:

Who: This training applies to all employees who operate Derricks. Operators shall be directed only by the individual specifically trained for that purpose. No derrick shall be loaded beyond the rated load.

When: No specific training time is mentioned in the OSHA standard.

OSHA standard §1910.183 applies only to helicopter crane operations.

If employees operate Helicopters then §1910.183.

Training Applies To:

Who: This training applies to all employees who operate helicopters. Ground personnel shall be instructed and the employer shall ensure that when visibility is reduced by dust or other conditions, they shall exercise special caution to keep clear of main and stabilizing rotors. Precautions shall also be taken by the employer to eliminate, as far as practical, the dust or other conditions reducing the visibility.

The employer shall instruct the aircrew and ground personnel on the signal systems to be used and shall review the system with the employees in advance of hoisting the load. This applies to both radio and hand signal systems.

No employee shall be permitted to approach within 50 feet of the helicopter when the rotor blades are turning, unless his work duties require his presence in that area.

When: The employer shall instruct employees, and shall ensure that whenever approaching or leaving a helicopter which has its blades rotating, all employees shall remain in full view of the pilot and keep in a crouched position. No employee shall be permitted to work in the area from the cockpit or cabin rearward while blades are rotating, unless authorized by the helicopter operator to work there.

Figure 5.13. Subpart O – Machinery and Machine Guarding

Subpart O – Machinery and Machine Guarding Training Requirements	
1910.217	Mechanical power presses
1910.218	Forging machines

Subpart O contains training requirements for particular kinds of machinery.

If employees operate Machinery then Mechanical Power Presses §1910.217.

Training Applies To:

Who: The training applies to all employees' who operate mechanical power presses and maintenance personnel. The employer shall train and instruct the operator in the safe method of work before starting work on any operation. The employer shall insure by adequate supervision that correct operating procedures are being followed.

Training of Maintenance Personnel

It shall be the responsibility of the employer to insure the original and continuing competence of personnel caring for, inspecting, and maintaining power presses.

Operator Training

The operator training shall be provided to the employee before the employee initially operates the press and as needed to maintain competence, but not less than annually thereafter. It shall include instruction relative to the following items for presses used in the PSDI mode and the following:

- The manufacturers recommended test procedures for checking operation of the presence sensing device. This shall include the use of the test rod required by this section;
- The safety distance required;
- The operation, function, and performance of the PSDI mode;
- The requirements for hand tools that may be used in the PSDI mode;
- The severe consequences that can result if he or she attempts to circumvent or by-pass any of the safeguard or operating functions of the PSDI system; and
- The employer shall certify that employees have been trained by preparing a certification record which includes the identity of the person trained, the signature of the employer or the person who conducted the training, and the date the training was completed. The certification record shall be prepared at the completion of the training and be maintained on file for the duration of the employee's employment. The certification record shall be made available to the Assistant Secretary for Occupational Safety and Health.

If employees operate Machinery then Forging Machines §1910.218.

Training Applies To:

Who: The training applies to all employees' who operate it. It shall be the responsibility of the employer to maintain all forge shop equipment in a condition which will ensure continued safe operation. This responsibility includes:

- Training personnel for the proper inspection, and
- Maintenance of forging machinery and equipment.

When: Training will be annually.

Figure 5.15. Subpart Q – Welding, Cutting and Brazing

Subpart Q – Welding, Cutting and Brazing Training Requirements	
1910.252	General requirements
1910.253	Oxygen-fuel gas welding and cutting
1910.254	Arc welding and cutting
1910.255	Resistance welding

Subpart Q regulates welding, cutting and brazing.

The general training requirements for welding, cutting and brazing are covered in §1910.252 and contain specific rules for fire prevention, protection of personnel, health protection and ventilation (particularly when substances such as fluorine compounds, lead, beryllium, cadmium, cleaning compounds and stainless steels are involved), and industrial applications.

Training Applies To:

Who: This training applies to all welders and cutters. Management shall recognize its responsibility for the safe usage of cutting and welding equipment on its property and insist that cutters or welders and their supervisors are suitably trained in the safe operation of their equipment and the safe use of fire extinguishing equipment.

When: There is no training time mentioned in the OSHA standard for training employees.

The remaining three training requirements are restricted to the particular operations listed below:

- Oxygen-fuel gas welding and cutting §1910.253,
- Arc welding and cutting §1910.254, and
- Resistance welding §1910.255.

Who: This training applies to all welders and cutters who operate Oxygen-fuel gas welding and cutting equipment.

Workmen in charge of the oxygen or fuel-gas supply equipment, including generators, and oxygen or fuel- gas distribution piping systems shall be instructed by their employers for his/her important work before being left in charge. Rules and instructions covering the operation and maintenance of oxygen or fuel-gas supply equipment including generators, and oxygen or fuel-gas distribution piping systems shall be readily available.

When: Training will be prior before the employee is left in charge.

Who: This training program applies to workmen designated to operate arc welding equipment. They shall be properly instructed and qualified to operate equipment.

When: Training will be prior to or at the time of initial assignment.

Who: This training program applies to workmen designated to operate resistance welding equipment. They shall be properly instructed and judged competent to operate equipment.

When: Training will be prior to or at the time of initial assignment.

Figure 5.16. Subpart R – Special Industries

Subpart R – Special Industries Training Requirements	
1910.261	Pulp, paper, and paperboard mills
1910.264	Laundry machinery and operations
1910.266	Logging operations
1910.268	Telecommunications
1910.269	Electrical power generation, transmission and distribution
1910.272	Grain handling facilities

There are six training requirements contained in Subpart R Special Industries.

If you have employees who work in the Pulp, Paper, and Paperboard Mills then OSHA standard §1910.261.

Training Applies To:

Who: The training applies to all employees exposed to chlorine gas. Gas masks capable of absorbing chlorine shall be supplied, conveniently placed, and regularly inspected, and workers who may be exposed to chlorine gas shall be instructed in their use.

When: Training shall be prior to or at the time of initial assignment.

If you have employees who work with Laundry Machinery and Operations then OSHA standard §1910.264.

Training Applies To:

Who: This training applies to all employees who operate laundry machines. Employees shall be properly instructed as to the hazards of their work and be instructed in safe practices, by bulletins, printed rules, and verbal instructions.

When: Training shall be at the time of initial assignment.

If you have employees who work with Logging Operations then §1910.266.

Training Applies To:

Who: The training applies to all employees who operate logging operations. Chain saw operators shall be instructed to inspect the saws daily to assure that all handles and guards are in place and tight, that all controls function properly, and that the muffler is operative.

- Chain saw operators shall be instructed to follow manufacturer's instructions as to operation and adjustment;
- Chain saw operators shall be instructed to fuel the saw only in safe areas and not under conditions conducive to fire such as near men smoking, hot engine;
- Chain saw operators shall be instructed to hold the saw with both hands during operations;
- Chain saw operators shall be instructed to start the saw at least 10 feet away from fueling area;
- Chain saw operators shall be instructed to start the saw only on the ground or when otherwise firmly supported;
- Chain saw operators shall be instructed to be certain of footing and to clear away brush which might interfere before starting to cut;

- Chain saw operators shall be instructed not to use engine fuel for starting fires or as a cleaning solvent;
- Chain saw operators shall be instructed to shut off the saw when carrying it for a distance greater than from tree to tree or in hazardous conditions such as slippery surfaces or heavy underbrush. The saw shall be at idle speed when carried short distances;
- Chain saw operators shall be instructed to carry the saw in a manner to prevent contact with the chain and muffler;
- Chain saw operators shall be instructed not to use the saw to cut directly overhead or at a distance that would require the operator to relinquish a safe grip on the saw;
- Equipment operators shall be instructed as to the manufacturer's recommendations for equipment operation, maintenance, safe practices, and site operating procedures;
- Equipment shall be kept free of flammable material;
- Equipment shall be kept free of any material which might contribute to slipping and falling;
- Engine of equipment shall be shut down during fueling, servicing, and repairs except where operation is required for adjustment;
- Equipment shall be inspected for evidence of failure or incipient failure;
- The equipment operator shall be instructed to walk completely around machine and assure that no obstacles or personnel are in the area before startup;
- The equipment operator shall be instructed to start and operate equipment only from the operator's station or from safe area recommended by the manufacturer;
- Seat belt shall be provided on mobile equipment;

- The equipment operator shall be instructed to check controls for proper function and response before starting working cycle;
- The equipment operator shall be instructed to ground or secure all movable elements when not in use;
- The equipment operator shall be advised of the load capacity and operating speed of the equipment;
- The equipment operator shall be advised of the stability limitations of the equipment;
- The equipment operator shall be instructed to maintain adequate distance from other equipment and personnel;
- Where signalmen are used, the equipment operator shall be instructed to operate the equipment only on signal designated signalman and only when signal is distinct and clearly understood;
- The equipment operator shall be instructed not to operate movable elements (boom, grapple, load, etc.) close to or over personnel;
- The equipment operator shall be instructed to signal his intention before operation when personnel are in or near the working area;
- The equipment operator shall be instructed to dismount and stand clear for all loading and unloading of his mobile vehicle by other mobile equipment. The dismounted operator shall be visible to loader operator;
- The equipment operator shall be instructed to operate equipment in a manner that will not place undue shock loads on wire rope;
- The equipment operator shall be instructed not to permit riders or observers on the machine unless approved seating and protection is provided;
- The equipment operator shall be instructed to shut down the engine when the equipment is

stopped, apply brake locks and ground moving elements before he dismounts;

- The equipment operator shall be instructed, when any equipment is transported from one job to another, to transport it on a vehicle of sufficient rated capacity and the equipment shall be properly secured during transit;
- Only trained and experienced personnel shall handle or use explosives. Usage shall comply with the requirements of §1910.109;
- The feller shall be instructed to plan retreat path and clear path as necessary before cut is started; and
- The feller shall be instructed to appraise situation for dead limbs, the lean of tree to be cut, wind conditions, location of trees and other hazards, and exercise proper precautions before cut is started.

When: The employer shall provide training for each employee, including supervisors, at no cost to the employee. Training shall be provided as follows:

- As soon as possible for initial training for each current and new employee;
- Prior to initial assignment for each new employee and whenever the employee is assigned new work tasks, tools, equipment, machines, or vehicles and;
- Whenever an employee demonstrates unsafe job performance and
- Training shall consist of the following elements:

    ✓ Safe performance of assigned work tasks;
    ✓ Safe use, operation, and maintenance of tools, machines, and vehicles the employees uses or operates, including emphasis on understanding and following

the manufacturer's instructions, warnings, and precautions;

✓ Recognition of safety and health hazards associated with the employee's specific work tasks, including the use of measures and work practices to prevent or control those hazards;

✓ Recognition, prevention, and control of other   safety and health hazards in the logging industry; and

✓ Procedures, practices, and requirements of the employer's work site.

Training of an employee due to unsafe job performance, or assignment of new work tasks, tools, equipment, machines, or vehicles may be limited to those elements which are relevant to the circumstances giving rise to the need for training.

Each current employee who has received training in the particular elements of there job shall not be required to be retrained in those elements. Each new employee who has received training in the particular elements specified shall not be required to be retrained in those elements prior to initial assignment.

The employer shall train each current and new employee in those elements for which the employee has not received training. The employer is responsible for ensuring that each current and new employee can properly and safely perform the work tasks and operate the tools, equipment, machines, and vehicles used in their job.

Each new employee who is required to be trained shall work under the close supervision of a designated person until the employee demonstrates to the employer the ability to safely perform the new duties independently.

The employer shall assure that each employee, including supervisors, receives or has received first-aid and CPR training as follows:

- The employer shall assure that each employee receives first-aid training at least every three years and receives CPR training at least annually;
- The employer shall assure that each employee's first-aid and CPR training and/or certificate of training remain current; and
- All training shall be conducted by a designated person and;
- The employer shall assure that all training required is presented in a manner that the employee is able to understand. The employer shall assure that all training materials used are appropriate in content and vocabulary to the educational level, literacy, and language skill of the employees being trained.

If you have employees who work in Telecommunications Operations then §1910.268.

Training Applies To:

Who: The training applies to all employees who work in telecommunications operations including the following: pole climbers, employees working on ladders, derricks, high voltage, manholes, and tree working operations. Employers assigned to work with storage batteries shall be instructed in emergency procedures such as dealing with accidental acid spills.

When: Employers shall provide training in the various precautions and safe practices and insure that employees do not engage in any activities until employees have received proper training. However, where the employer can demonstrate that an employee is already trained in the precautions and safe practices training need not by provided to that employee.

Where training is required, it shall consist of on-the-job training or classroom-type training or a combination of both. The employer shall certify that employees have been trained by preparing a certification record which includes the identity of the person trained, the signature of the employer or the person who conducted the training, and the date the training was completed.

The certification record shall be prepared at the completion of training and shall be maintained on file for the duration of the employee's employment. The certification record shall be made available upon request to the Assistant Secretary for Occupational Safety and Health. Training shall include the following:

- Recognition and avoidance of dangers relating to encounters with harmful substances and animal, insect, or plant life;
- Procedures to be followed in emergency situations; and
- First-aid training including instruction in artificial respiration.

Derrick Trucks Training

Only persons trained in the operation of the derrick shall be permitted to operate the derrick.

Cable Fault Training

Employees involved in using high voltages to locate trouble or test cables shall be instructed in the precautions necessary for their own safety and the safety of the employees.

Guarding Manholes Training

While work is being performed in the manhole, a person with basic first-aid training shall be immediately available to render assistance if there is cause for believing that a safety hazard exists, and if the requirements do not adequately protect the employee(s).

Joint Power and Telecommunication Manholes Training

While work is being performed in a manhole occupied jointly by an electric utility and a telecommunication utility, an employee with a basic first-aid training shall be available in the immediate vicinity to render emergency assistance may be required.

The employee whose presence is required in the immediate vicinity for the purposes of the rendering emergency assistance is not to be precluded from occasionally entering a manhole to provide assistance other than in an emergency. The requirement does not preclude a qualified employee, working alone, from entering for brief periods of time, a manhole where energized cables or equipment are in service, for the purpose of inspection, housekeeping, taking readings, or similar work if work can be performed safely.

Tree Trimming Training

Employees engaged in line-clearing operations shall be instructed in the following:

- A direct contact is made when any part of the body touches or contacts an energized conductor, or other energized electrical fixture or apparatus;
- An indirect contact is made when any part of the body touches any object in contact with an energized electrical conductor, or other energized fixture or apparatus;
- An indirect contact can be made through conductive tools, tree branches, trucks, equipment, or other objects, or as a result of

> communications wires, cables, fences, or guy wires being accidentally energized; and

- Electric shock will occur when an employee, by either direct of indirect contact with an energized conductor, energized tree limb, tool, equipment, or other object, provides a path for the flow of electricity to a grounded object or to the ground itself. Simultaneous contact with two energized conductors will also cause electric shock which may result in serious or fatal injury.

Only qualified employees or trainees, familiar with the special techniques and hazards involved in line clearance, shall be permitted to perform the work if it is found that an electrical hazard exists.

During tree working operations where an electrical hazard of more than 750V exists, there shall be a second employee or trainee qualified in line clearance tree trimming within normal voice communication.

If you have employees who work with Electric Power Generation, Transmission, and Distribution Operations then §1910.269.

Training Applies To:

Who: This training applies to all employees who operate generation transmission and distribution of electric utilities. The employer shall provide medical services and first aid training as required by the OSHA standard §1910.151. In addition, the following requirements also apply:

> When employees are performing work on or associated with exposed lines or equipment energized at 50 volts or more, persons trained in first aid including cardiopulmonary resuscitation (CPR) shall be available as follows:
>
> - For field work involving two or more employees at a work location, at least two trained persons shall be

available. However, only one trained person need be available if all new employees are trained in first aid, including CPR, within 3 months of their hiring dates; and

- For fixed work locations such as generating stations, the number of trained persons available shall be sufficient to ensure that each employee exposed to electric shock can be reached within 4 minutes by a trained person. However, where the existing number of employees is insufficient to meet this requirement (at a remote substation, for example), all employees at the work location shall be trained.

The employer shall also provide training to ensure that the purpose and function of the energy control program are understood by employees and that the knowledge and skills required for the safe applications, usage, and removal of energy controls are acquired by employees. The training shall include the following:

- Each authorized employee shall receive training in the recognition of applicable hazardous energy sources, the type and magnitude of energy available in the workplace, and in the methods and means necessary for energy isolation and control;
- Each affected employees shall be instructed in the purpose of the use of the energy control procedure;
- All other employees whose work operations are or may be in an area where energy control procedures may be used shall be instructed about the procedures and about the prohibition relating to attempts to restart or reenergize machines or equipment that are locked out of tagged out;
- When tagout systems are used, employees shall also be trained in the limitation of tags; and
- Retraining shall be provided by the employer as follows:

When: Retraining shall be provided for all authorized and affected employees whenever there is a change in their job assignments, a change in machines, equipment, or processes that present a new hazard or whenever there is a change in the energy control procedures.

Retraining shall also be conducted whenever a periodic inspection reveals, or whenever the employer has reason to believe, there are deviations form or inadequacies in an employee's knowledge or use of the energy control procedures.

The retraining shall establish employee proficiency and shall introduce new or revised control methods and procedures, as necessary.

If employees are involved in Grain Handling Facilities then OSHA standard §1910.272.

Training Applies To:

Who: This training applies to all employers who are involved in handling grain.

When: The employer shall provide training to employees at least annually and when changes in job assignment will expose them to new hazards. Current employees, and new employees prior to starting work, shall be trained in the following:

- General safety precautions associated with the facility, including recognition and preventive measures for the hazards related to dust accumulations and common ignition sources such as smoking;

- Specific procedures and safety practices applicable to their job tasks including but not limited to, cleaning procedures for grinding equipment, clearing procedures for choked legs, housekeeping procedures, hot work procedures, preventive maintenance procedures and lock-out/tag-out procedures; and

- Employees assigned special tasks, such as bin entry and handling of flammable or toxic substances shall be provided training to perform these tasks safely.

Entry into Bins, Silos, and Tanks

The employee acting as observer shall be trained in rescue procedures, including notification methods for obtaining additional assistance.

Contractors

The employer shall explain the applicable provisions of the emergency action plan to contractors.

Figure 5.17. Subpart S – Electrical

Subpart S – Electrical Training Requirements	
SAFETY-RELATED WORK PRACTICES	
1910.331	Scope
1910.332	Training
1910.333	Selection and use of work practices
1910.334	Use of equipment
1910.335	Safeguards for personnel protection

The Subpart S training requirements apply to all electrical equipment and installations that are used to provide electrical power and light for places, buildings, structures and other premises where employees work, including yards, industrial substations, conductors that connect the installations to a supply of electricity.

Safety-related Work Practices are the regulations covering the practices and procedures that must be observed in order to protect employees who are working on or near exposed energized and deenergized parts of electric equipment.

All employees who face a risk of electric shock, burns or other related injuries that are not reduced to a safe level by the installation safety requirements of Subpart S, must be trained in the safety-related work practices required by OSHA standards §1910.331 through §1910.335.

In addition to being trained in and familiar with safety related work practices some employees must also be trained in the inherent hazards of electricity, such as high voltages, electric current, arcing, grounding, and lack of guarding. Any electrically related safety practices not specifically addressed by OSHA standards §1910.331 through §1910.335, but necessary for safety in specific workplace conditions, must be included in the training.

If employees are exposed to Electrical Hazards then OSHA standards §1910.331-§1910.335.

Training Applies To:

Who: This training applies to all employees exposed to the dangers of electrical hazards. Employees shall be trained in and familiar with the safety-related work practices that pertain to their respective job assignments.

When: The training required shall be of the classroom or on-the-job type. The degree of training provided shall be determined by the risk to the employee. Qualified persons (i.e. those permitted to work on or near exposed energized parts) shall, at a minimum, be trained in the following:

- The skills and techniques necessary to distinguish

exposed live parts from other parts of electric equipment;
- The skills and techniques necessary to determine the nominal voltage of exposed live parts; and
- The clearance distances and the corresponding voltages to which the qualified person will be exposed.

Figure 5.18. Subpart T – Commercial Diving Operations

Subpart T – Commercial Diving Operations Training Requirements	
1910.410	Qualifications of dive team

Subpart T applies to diving and related support operations conducted in connection with all types of work involved with commercial diving operations.

If you have employees who work in Commercial Diving Operations then OSHA standard §1910.410.

Training Applies To:

Each dive team member shall have the experience or training necessary to perform assigned tasks in a safe and healthful manner. Each dive team member shall have the experience or training in the following:

- The use of tools, equipment, and systems relevant to assigned tasks;
- Techniques of the assigned diving mode; and;
- Diving operations and emergency procedures.

All dive team members shall be trained in cardiopulmonary resuscitation and first aid (American Red Cross standard course or equivalent).

Dive team members who are exposed to or control the exposure of others to hyperbaric conditions shall be trained in diving-related physics and physiology.

Each dive team member shall be assigned tasks in accordance with the employee's experience or training, except that limited additional tasks may be assigned to an employees undergoing training provided that these tasks are performed under the direct supervision of an experienced dive team member.

Designated Person-in-Charge

The designated person-in-charge shall have experience and training in the conduct of the assigned diving operations.

Figure 5.20. Subpart Z – Toxic and Hazardous Substances

Subpart Z – Toxic and Hazardous Substances Training Requirements	
1910.1000	Air contaminants
1910.1001	Asbestos
1910.1002	Coal tar pitch volatiles
1910.1003	13 Carcinogens – (4-Nitrobiphenyl, etc.)
1910.1004	Alpha-Naphthylamine
1910.1006	Methyl chloromethyl ether
1910.1007	3,3' - Dichlorobenzidine (and its salts)
1910.1008	Bis-Chloromethyl ether
1910.1009	Beta-Naphthylamine
1910.1010	Benzidine
1910.1011	4-Aminodiphenyl
1910.1012	Ethyleneimine
1910.1013	Beta-Propiolactone
1910.1014	2-Acetylaminofluorene
1910.1015	4-Dimethylaminoazobenzene
1910.1016	N-Nitrosodimethylamine
1910.1017	Vinyl chloride

Subpart Z – Toxic and Hazardous Substances Training Requirements (Continued)	
1910.1018	Inorganic arsenic
1910.1025	Lead
1910.1027	Cadmium
1910.1028	Benzene
1910.1029	Coke oven emissions
1910.1030	Bloodborne pathogens
1910.1043	Cotton dust
1910.1044	1,2-dibromo-3 chloropropane
1910.1045	Acrylonitrile
1910.1047	Ethylene oxide
1910.1048	Formaldehyde
1910.1050	Methylenedianiline
1910.1051	1, 3-butadiene
1910.1052	Methylene Chloride
1910.1096	Ionizing radiation
1910.1200	Hazard communication
1910.1450	Occupational exposure to hazardous chemicals in laboratories

The Subpart Z standards set airborne permissible exposure limits (PEL's) for over 450 listed substances.

They impose a number of specific training requirements to be implemented in workplaces where those substances are present, and require employers, chemical manufacturers and importers, to provide information upon all hazardous chemicals through a variety of specified methods.

A PEL is the maximum amount of a contaminant in the air to which workers may be exposed to over a given period of time.

§1910.1000, Air contaminants lists 428 substances that literally cover the alphabet from Acetaldehyde to Zirconium and sets a PEL for each of them. Employers are required to keep those substances within the PEL if it is feasible to do so or, if not, require exposed employees to use personal protective equipment that keeps their exposure within the listed PEL.

§1910.1001 through §1910.1052 are limited to the single substance listed in each standard's title. Those standards impose additional requirements that are not included in §1910.1000.

If any of your employees could be exposed to any of the substances covered by the standards in §1910.1001 through §1910.1052, you must familiarize yourself with the relevant training requirements.

You should determine whether any of them are present in your workplace and, if so, whether the airborne level of each such substance is within the specified PEL. If the listed PEL is not exceeded, you have no need to be concerned with §1910.1000. If it is exceeded, you must familiarize yourself with that standard and take the measures specified in §1910.1000.

Do employees perform work where they may be exposed to Asbestos then OSHA standard §1910.1001.

Training Applies To:

Who: The employer shall institute a training program for all employees who are exposed to airborne concentrations of asbestos at or above the PEL and/or excursion limit and ensure their participation in the program.

When: Training shall be provided prior to or at the time of initial assignment and at least annually thereafter. The training program shall be conducted in a manner which the employee is able to understand.

The employer shall also provide at no cost to employees who perform housekeeping operations in an area which contains ACM or PACM, an asbestos awareness training course, which shall contain the following elements: health effects of asbestos, locations of ACM and PACM in the building/facility, recognition of ACM and PACM damage and deterioration, requirements in this standard relating to housekeeping, and proper response to fiber release episodes, to all employees who perform housekeeping work in areas where ACM and/or PACM is present.

Each employee shall be trained at least once a year on the following:

- Health effects of asbestos;
- The relationship between smoking, asbestos, and increased risk of lung cancer;
- How quantity, location, manner of use, release, and storage of asbestos could result in exposure to asbestos;
- The engineering controls and work practices for reducing asbestos exposure;
- The proper procedures to be followed to reduce the risk of exposure;
- A description of the medical surveillance program;
- The OSHA standard asbestos labeling and posting requirements; and

- Where to get additional information and
- The proper use of respirators and protective clothing.

If employees are exposed to Toxic and Hazardous Substances - (13 Carcinogens) then

Training Applies To:

- 4-Nitrobiphenyl – §1910.1003
- Alpha-Naphthylamine – §1910.1004
- Methyl chloromethyl ether –§1910.1006
- 3,3'-Dichlorobenzidine (and its salts) – §1910.1007
- Bis-Chloromethyl ether – §1910.1008
- Beta-Naphthylamine – §1910.1009
- Benzidine – §1910.1010
- 4-Aminodiphenyl – §1910.1011
- Ethyleneimine – §1910.1012
- Beta-Propiolactone – §1910.1013
- 2-Acetylaminofluorene -§1910.1014
- 4 Dimethylaminoazobenezen-§1910.1015 and
- N-Nitrosodimethylamine – §1910.1016

Training Applies To:

Who: This training applies to all authorized employees who perform work where they may be exposed to the 13 carcinogens which are manufactured, processed, repackaged, released, handled, or stored, but shall not apply to transshipment in sealed containers.

Authorized employees means those employees assigned to work where a regulated chemical is manufactured, processed, used, repackaged, released, handled, or stored.

When: Each employee prior to being authorized to enter a regulated area shall receive a training and indoctrination program including the following:

- The nature of the carcinogenic hazards of a carcinogen addressed by this section, including local and systemic toxicity;
- The specific nature of the operation involving the listed substances which could result in exposure;
- The purpose for and application of the medical surveillance program, including, as appropriate, methods of self-examination;
- The purpose for an application of decontamination practices and purposes;
- The purpose for and significance of emergency practices and procedures;
- The employee's specific role in emergency procedures;
- Specific information to aid the employee in recognition and evaluation of conditions and situations which may result in the release of 4-Nitrobiphenyl;
- The purpose for and application of specific first aid procedures and practices;
- A review of the training section at the employee's first training and indoctrination program and annually thereafter.

Specific emergency procedures shall be prescribed, and posted, and employees shall be familiarized with their terms, and rehearsed in their application.

Are employees exposed to Vinyl Chloride then §1910.1017.

Training Applies To:

Who: This training applies to each employee engaged in vinyl chloride or polyvinyl chloride operations shall be provided training in a program relating to the hazards of vinyl chloride and precautions for its safe use. The program should include:

- The nature of the health hazard from chronic exposure to vinyl chloride including specifically the carcinogenic hazard;
- The specific nature of operations which could result in exposure to vinyl chloride in excess of the permissible limit and necessary protective steps;
- The purpose for, proper use, and limitations of respiratory protective devices;
- The fire hazard and acute toxicity of vinyl chloride, and the necessary protective steps;
- The purpose for and a description of the monitoring program;
- The purpose for, and a description of, the medical surveillance program; and
- Specific information to aid the employee in recognition of conditions which may result in the release of vinyl chloride.

When: Employees must be trained at the first training and indoctrination program, and annually thereafter.

Are employees exposed to Inorganic Arsenic then §1910.1018.

Training Applies To:

Who: This training applies to all employees who are subject to exposure to inorganic arsenic above the action level without regard to respirator use, or for whom there is a possibility of skin or eye irritation form inorganic arsenic. The employer shall assure that those employees participate in the training program.

When: The training program shall be provided for all employees at the time of initial assignment for those subsequently covered by this standard, and shall be repeated at least quarterly for employees who have optional use of respirators and at least annually for other covered employees thereafter, and the employer shall assure that each employee is informed of the following:

- The quantity, location, manner of use, storage, sources of exposure, and the specific nature of operations which could result in exposure to inorganic arsenic as well as any necessary protective steps;
- The purpose, proper use, and limitation of respirators;
- The purpose and a description of the medical surveillance program,
- The engineering controls and work practices associated with the employee's job assignment; and

The employer shall make available to all affected employees a copy of this standard, its appendices and provide upon request all materials relating to the employee information and training program to the Assistant Secretary and the Director.

Do employees perform work where they may be exposed to Lead then §1910.1025.

Training Applies To:

Who: Each employer who has a workplace in which there is a potential exposure to airborne lead at any level shall inform employees of the content of this regulation.

The employer shall institute a training program for and assure the participation of all employees who are subject to exposure to lead at or above the action level of for whom the possibility of skin or eye irritation exists.

When: The employer shall provide initial training prior to the time of initial job assignment for employees covered by this standard. The training program shall be repeated at least annually for each employee and assure that each employee is informed of the following:

- The content of this standard and its appendices;

- The specific nature of the operations which could result in exposure to lead above the action level;
- The purpose, proper selection, fitting, use, and limitations of respirators;
- The purpose and a description of the medical surveillance program, and the medical removal protection program including information concerning the adverse health effects associated with excessive exposure to lead (with particular attention to the adverse reproductive effects on both males and females);
- The engineering controls and work practices associated with the employee's job assignment;
- The contents of any compliance plan in effect; and
- Instruction to employees that chelating agents should not routinely be used to remove lead form their bodies and should not be used at all except under the direction of a licensed physician.

The employer shall make readily available to all affected employees a copy of this standard and its appendices. The employer shall provide, upon request, all materials relating to the employee information and training program to the Assistant Secretary and the Director.

Are employees exposed to Cadmium then OSHA standard §1910.1027.

Training Applies To:

Who: The employer shall institute a training program for all employees who are potentially exposed to cadmium, assure employee participation in the program, and maintain a record of the contents of the program.

When: Training shall be provided prior to or at the time of initial assignment to a job involving potential exposure to cadmium and at least annually. The employer shall make the training program understandable to the employee and assure that each employee is informed of the following:

- The health hazards associated with cadmium exposure, with special attention to the information incorporated in appendix A of the standard;
- The quantity, location, manner of use, release, and storage of cadmium in the workplace and the specific nature of operations that could result in exposure to cadmium, especially exposures above the permissible exposure limits (PELs);
- The engineering and work practices associated with the employee's job assignment;
- The measures employees can take to protect themselves from exposure to cadmium, including modification of such habits as smoking and personal hygiene, and specific procedures the employer has implemented to protect employees from exposure to cadmium such as appropriate work practices, emergency procedures, and the provision of personal protective equipment;
- The purpose, proper selection, fitting, proper use, and limitations of respirators and protective clothing;
- The purpose and a description of the medical surveillance programs training section;

The employer shall make a copy of this training section and its appendices readily available without cost to all affected employees and shall provide a copy if requested.

Are employees exposed to Benzene then §1910.1028.

Training Applies To:

Who: This training applies to all employees who are exposed to benzene.

When: The employer shall provide employees with information and training at the time of their initial assignment to a work area where benzene is present. If exposures are above the action level, employees shall be provided with information and training at least annually thereafter.

The training program shall be in accordance with the requirements of the Hazard Communication program, and include specific information on benzene for each category of information included.

The employer shall also provide employees with an explanation of the contents of this training section, including Appendices A and B, and indicate to them where the standard is available; and, describe the medical surveillance program.

Are employees exposed to Coke Oven Emissions then §1910.1029.

Training Applies To:

Who: The employer shall institute a training program for all employees exposed to coke oven emissions in the regulated area and shall assure their participation.

When: The training program shall be provided at the time of initial assignment and at least annually for all employees who are employed in the regulated area, except that training regarding the occupational safety and health hazards associated with exposure to coke oven emissions and the purpose, proper use, and limitations of respiratory protective devices shall be provided at least quarterly, The training program shall include informing each employee of:

- The information contained in the substance information sheet for coke oven emissions;
- The purpose, proper use, and limitations of respiratory protective devices ;and
- The purpose for and a description of the medical surveillance program including information on the occupational safety and health hazards associated with exposure to coke oven emissions.

The employer shall make a copy of this standard and its appendices readily available to all employees who are employed in the regulated area.

If there are areas in the workplace where employees could have occupational exposure to blood or other ootentially infectious Materials then Bloodborne Pathogens §1910.1030.

Training Applies To:

Who: All employees with occupational exposure must participate in a training program which will be provided at no cost to affected employees during normal working hours.

When: The training will be provided at the time of initial assignment to tasks where occupational exposure may take place and at least annually thereafter.

For employees who have received training on bloodborne pathogens in the year preceding the effective date of the OSHA standard, only training with respect to the provisions of the standard which were not included need be provided.

Annual training for all employees will be provided within one year of their previous training.

Additional training will be provided when changes such as modification of tasks or procedures or institution of new tasks or procedures affect the employee's occupational exposure. The additional training may be limited to addressing the new exposures created. Material appropriate in content and vocabulary to educational level, literacy, and language of employees will be used.

The training program will contain the following:

- An accessible copy of the regulatory text of the OSHA bloodborne pathogens standard and an explanation of its contents;

- A general explanation of the epidemiology and symptoms of bloodborne diseases;
- An explanation of the modes of transmissions of bloodborne pathogens;
- An explanation of the exposure control plan and the means by which the employee can obtain a copy;
- An explanation of the appropriate methods for recognizing tasks and other activities that may involve exposure to blood and other potentially infectious materials;
- An explanation of the use and limitations of methods that will prevent or reduce exposure including appropriate engineering controls, work practices, and personal protective equipment;
- Information on the types, proper use, location, removal, handling, decontamination and disposal of personal protective equipment;
- Information on the hepatitis B vaccine, including the benefits of being vaccinated, and that the vaccine and vaccination will be offered free of charge;
- Information on the appropriate actions to take and person to contact in an emergency involving blood or other potentially infectious materials;
- An explanation of the procedure to follow if an exposure incident occurs, including the method of reporting the incident and the medical follow-up that will be made available;
- Information on the post-exposure evaluation and follow-up that we are required to provide for the employee following an exposure incident;
- An explanation of the signs and labels and/or color coding required by the OSHA bloodborne pathogens standard;
- An opportunity for interactive questions and answers with the person conducting the training session; and
- The person conducting the training will be knowledgeable in the subject matter covered by

the elements contained in the training program as it relates to the particular work place that the training will address.

Training records will be maintained for three years from the date on which the training occurred and include the following:

- Dates of training sessions;
- Contents or summary of training program, including the trainers name and qualifications; and
- Job titles and names of all persons attending the training session.

Are employees exposed to Cotton Dust then §1910.1043.

Training Applies To:

Who: The employer shall provide a training program for all employees exposed to cotton dust and shall assure that each employee is informed of the following:

- The acute and long-term health hazards associated with exposure to cotton dust;
- The names and descriptions of jobs and processes which could result in exposure to cotton dust at or above the permissible exposure levels;
- The measures, including work practices of the standard, necessary to protect the employee from exposures in excess of the permissible exposure limit;
- The purpose, proper use and limitations of respirators;
- The purpose for and a description of the medical surveillance program and other information which will aid exposed employees in understanding the hazards of cotton dust exposure; and
- The contents of the standard and its appendices.

When: The training shall be provided prior to initial assignment and shall be repeated annually for each employee exposed to cotton dust, when job assignments or work processes change, and when employee performance indicates a need for retraining.

Each employer shall post a copy of this training section with its appendices in a public location at the workplace, and shall, upon request, make copies available to employees. The employer shall provide all materials relating to the employee training and information program to the Assistant Secretary and the Director upon request.

Are employees exposed to 1, 2-Dibromo-3-Chloropropane then §1910.1044.

Training Applies To:

Who: The employer shall institute a training program for all employees who may be exposed to DBCP and shall assure their participation in a training program. The employer shall assure that each employee is informed of the following:

- The quantity, location, manner of use, release or storage of DBCP and the specific nature of operations which could result in exposure to DBCP as well as any necessary protective steps;
- The purpose, proper use, and limitations of respirators and;
- The purpose and description of the medical surveillance program.

When: The employer shall make a copy of this standard and its appendices available to all affected employees. The employer shall provide, upon request, all materials relating to the employee information and training program to the Assistant Secretary and the Director.

Are employees exposed to Acrylonitrile then §1910.1045.

Training Applies To:

Who: The employer shall institute a training program for and assure the participation of all employees exposed to AN above the action level, all employees whose exposures are maintained below the action level by engineering and work practice controls, and all employees subject to potential skin or eye contact with liquid AN.

When: Training shall be provided at the time of initial assignment, or upon institution of the training program, and at least annually thereafter, and the employer shall assure that each employee is informed of the following:

- The quantity, location, manner of use, release, or storage of AN, and the specific nature of operations which could result in exposure to AN, as well as any necessary protective steps;
- The purpose, proper use, and limitations of respirators and protective clothing;
- The purpose and a description of the medical surveillance program;
- The emergency procedures developed; Engineering and work practice controls, their function, and the employee's relationship to these controls; and

The employer shall make a copy of this standard and its appendices readily available to all affected employees.

Are employees exposed to Ethylene Oxide then §1910.1047.

Training Applies To:

Who: This training applies to all employees who may be exposed to Ethylene Oxide and shall be informed of the following:

- Any operations in their work area where EtO is present;
- The location and availability of the written EtO final rule; and
- The medical surveillance program.

When: The employer shall provide employees who are potentially exposed to EtO at or above the action level with information and training on EtO at the time of initial assignment and at least annually thereafter.

Employer Training Shall Include the Following:

- Methods and observations that may be used to detect the presence or release of EtO in the work area (such as monitoring conducted by the employer, continuous monitoring devices, etc.);
- The physical and health hazards of EtO;
- The measures employees can take to protect themselves from hazards associated with EtO exposure, including specific procedures the employer has implemented to protect employees form exposure to EtO, such as work practices, emergency procedures, and personal protective equipment to be used; and
- The details of the hazard communication program developed by the employer, including an explanation of the labeling systems and how employees can obtain and use the appropriate hazard information.

Are employees exposed to Formaldehyde then §1910.1048.

Training Applies To:

Who: This training applies to all employees who are assigned to workplaces where there is exposure to formaldehyde, except where the employer can show, using objective data, that employees are not exposed to formaldehyde at of above 0.1 ppm, the employer is not required to provide training.

When: Employers shall provide information and training to employees at the time of initial assignment, and whenever a new exposure to formaldehyde is introduced into the work. The training shall be repeated at least annually.

The training program shall be conducted in a manner which the employee is able to understand and include:

- A discussion of the contents of this regulation and the contents of the Material Safety Data Sheet;
- The purpose for and a description of the medical surveillance program;
- A description of the potential health hazards associated with exposure to formaldehyde and a description of the signs and symptoms of exposure to formaldehyde;
- Instructions to immediately report to the employer the development of any adverse signs or symptoms that the employee suspect is attributable to formaldehyde exposure;
- Description of operations in the work area where formaldehyde is present and an explanation of the safe work practices appropriate for limiting exposure to formaldehyde in each job;
- The purpose for, proper use of, and limitations of personal protective clothing and equipment;
- Instructions for the handling of spills, emergencies, and clean-up procedures;
- An explanation of the importance of engineering and work practice controls for employee protection and any necessary instruction in the use of these controls; and
- A review of emergency procedures including the specific duties or assignments of each employee in the event of an emergency.

Do employees perform work where Methylenedianiline may be exposed then §1910.1050.

Training Applies To:

Who: The training applies to all employees in which there is exposure to Methylenedianiline. The employer shall also provide employees with information and training on MDA in accordance with the Hazard Communication standard 29 CFR §1910.1200(h) at the time of initial assignment and at least annually thereafter.

When: The employer shall provide an explanation of the contents of this standard, including appendices A and B, and indicate to employees where a copy of the standard is available and provide access to training materials and make available to all affected employees, without cost, all written materials relating to the employee training program, including a copy of this regulation; and describe the medical surveillance program required and explain the information contained in Appendix C and describe the medical removal provision required under paragraph (n) of this standard.

Do employees perform work where 1, 3-Butadiene may be exposed then §1910.1051.

Training Applies To:

Who: The employer shall communicate the hazards associated with BD exposure in accordance with the requirements of the Hazard Communication Standard, 29 CFR §1910.1200.

The employer shall provide all employees exposed to BD with information and training in accordance with the requirements of the Hazard Communication Standard, 29 CFR §1910.1200.

The employer shall institute a training program for all employees who are potentially exposed to BD at or above the action level or the STEL, ensure employee participation in the program and maintain a record of the contents of such program.

When: Training shall be provided prior to or at the time of initial assignment to a job potentially involving exposure to BD at or above the action level or STEL and at least annually thereafter.

The training program shall be conducted in a manner that the employee is able to understand. The employee shall ensure that each employee exposed to BD over the action level or STEL is informed of the following:

- The health hazards associated with BD exposure, and the purpose and a description of the medical screening and surveillance program;

- The quantity, location, manner of use, release, and storage of BD and the specific operations that could result in exposure to BD, especially exposures above the PEL or STEL;

- The engineering controls and work practices associated with the employee's job assignment, and emergency procedures and personal protective equipment;

- The measures employees can take to protect themselves from exposure to BD;

- The contents of this standard and its appendices; and

- The right of each employee exposed to BD at or above the action level or STEL to obtain medical examinations as required at no cost to the employee, the employee's medical records and all air monitoring results representing the employee's exposure to BD.

Access to Information and Training Materials

The employer shall make a copy of this standard and its appendices readily available without cost to all affected employees and their designated representatives and provide a copy if requested.

The employer shall provide to the Assistant Secretary or the Director, or the designated employee representatives, upon request, all materials relating to the employee information and the training program.

Are employees exposed to Methylene Chloride then §1910.1052.

Training Applies To:

Who: This training applies to all employees who have exposure to airborne concentrations of MC exceeds or can reasonably be expected to exceed the action level, the employer shall inform each affected employee of the quantity, location, manner of use, release, and storage of MC and the specific operations in the workplace that could result in exposure to MC, particularly noting where exposures may be above the 8-hour TWA PEL or STEL.

This program also applies to retraining affected employee as necessary to ensure that each employee exposed above the action level or the STEL maintains the requisite understanding of the principles of safe use and handling of MC in the workplace.

When: The employer shall provide information and training for each affected employee prior to or at the time of initial assignment to a job involving potential exposure to MC. The employer shall ensure that information and training is presented in a manner that is understandable to the employees.

The employer shall inform each affected employee of the requirements of this section and information available in its appendices, as well as how to access or obtain a copy of it in the workplace.

The employer shall retrain each affected employee as necessary to ensure that each employee exposed above the action level or the STEL maintains the requisite understanding of the principles of safe use and handling of MC in the workplace.

Whenever there are workplace changes, such as modifications of tasks or procedures or the institution of new tasks or procedures, which increase employee exposure, and where those exposures exceed or can reasonably be expected to exceed the action level, the employer shall update the training as necessary to ensure that each affected employee has the requisite proficiency.

An employer whose employees are exposed to MC at a multi-employer worksite shall notify the other employers with work operations at that site in accordance with the requirements of the Hazard Communication Standard, 29 CFR §1910.1200, as appropriate.

Does your facility have or use Radioactive Materials then Ionizing Radiation §1910.1096.

Training Applies To:

Who: The training program applies to all employees working in or frequenting any portion of a radiation area shall be informed of the occurrence of radioactive materials or of radiation in such portions of the radiation area; shall be instructed in the safety problems associated with exposure to such materials or radiation and in precautions or devices to minimize exposure; shall be instructed in the applicable provisions of this standard for the protection of employees from exposure to radiation or radioactive materials; and shall be advised of reports of radiation exposure which employees may request pursuant to the regulations in this section.

When: All employees whose work may necessitate their presence in an area covered by the signal shall be made familiar with the actual sound of the signal-preferably as it sounds at their work location. Before placing the system into operation, all employees normally working in the area shall be made acquainted with the signal by actual demonstration at their work locations.

Every employer must pay strict attention to §1910.1200, the Hazard Communication standard. It requires that chemical manufacturers and importers assess the hazards of all chemicals that they produce or import and furnish detailed information to their customers on those determined to be hazardous. It also requires all employers to provide that information to their employees by means of a written hazard communication program, labels on containers, material safety data sheets, employee training and access to written records and documents.

The term "hazardous chemical" is defined very broadly (for example, table salt is included) so virtually every employer is required to observe §1910.1200. It is also the most cited OSHA standard.

Are employees exposed to Hazardous Chemicals in the workplace then Hazard Communication §1910.1200.

Training Applies To:

Who: Employers shall provide all employees who are exposed to chemicals with information and training on hazardous chemicals in their work area.

When: The training shall be at the time of their initial assignment, and whenever a new physical or health hazard the employees have not previously been trained about is introduced into their work area. Information and training may be designed to cover categories of hazards (e.g., flammability, carcinogenicity) or specific chemicals. Chemical-specific information must always be available through labels and material safety data sheets.

Employees shall also be informed of the following:

- Any operations in their work area where hazardous chemicals are present;
- The location and availability of the written hazard communication program, including the required list(s) of hazardous chemicals, and material safety data sheets required by this section;
- Methods and observations that may be used to detect the presence or release of a hazardous chemical in the work area (such as monitoring conducted by the employer, continuous monitoring devices, visual appearance or odor of hazardous chemicals when being released, etc.);
- The physical and health hazards of the chemicals in the work area;
- The measures employees can take to protect themselves from these hazards, including specific procedures the employer has implemented to protect employees from exposure to hazardous chemicals, such as appropriate work practices, emergency procedures, and personal protective equipment to be used;
- The details of the hazard communication program developed by the employer, including an explanation of the labeling system and the material safety data sheet, and how employees can obtain and use the appropriate hazard information.

§1910.1450 is limited in its application to laboratories where hazardous chemicals are handled or used on a "laboratory scale".

Are employees exposed to Hazardous Chemicals in Laboratories then §1910.1450.

Training Applies To:

Who: This training program applies to all employees who works with or is potentially exposed to hazardous chemicals in laboratories.

When: Employees will receive initial training on the OSHA standard regulating occupational exposures to hazardous chemicals in laboratories and the safe use of those hazardous chemicals.

The training will cover all hazardous substances to which an employee may be exposed. A program that uses both audiovisual materials and classroom type training. Refresher training will be provided when needed. Whenever a new hazard is introduced, additional training will be provided.

Managers and other supervisors will be extensively trained regarding hazards and appropriate protective measures so they will be available to answer questions from employees and provide daily monitoring of safe work practices.

The training should emphasize the following items:

- Content of the OSHA laboratory standard and its appendices, an explanation of all of the provisions of the chemical hygiene plan, including its location and availability;
- Chemical and physical properties of hazardous materials (e.g., flash point, reactivity) and methods that can be used to detect the presence or release of chemicals (including chemicals in unlabeled pipes). This will include methods such as monitoring that we conduct continuous monitoring devices, visual appearance or odor of hazardous chemicals when being released;
- Physical hazards of chemicals (e.g., potential for fire, explosion;

- Health hazards, including signs and symptoms of exposure, associated with exposure to chemicals and any medical condition known to be aggravated by exposure to the chemical;
- The permissible exposure limits for OSHA regulated substances and the recommended exposure limits for other hazardous chemicals where there is no applicable OSHA standard;
- The measures that employees can take to protect themselves from these hazards, including the specific procedures that have been implemented here in order to protect our employees from exposure to hazardous chemicals, such as appropriate work practices, emergency procedures, and personal protective equipment to be used;
- Procedures to protect against hazards (e.g., personal protective equipment required, proper use and maintenance; work practices or methods to assure proper use and handling of chemicals; and procedures for emergency response);
- Work procedures to follow to assure protection when cleaning hazardous chemical spills and leaks;
- Where MSDS's are located, how to read and interpret the information on both container labels and MSDS's, and how employees may obtain additional hazard information;
- The location and availability of all other known reference materials on the hazards, safe handling, storage and disposal of hazardous chemicals found in the laboratory; and
- Prior approval protocols and procedures for handling select carcinogens, reproductive toxins, and substances with a high degree of acute toxicity.

The safety manager will regularly review the employee training program and advise on training or retraining needs as appropriate.

Retraining is required when the hazard changes or when a new hazard is introduced into the laboratory, but it will be company policy to provide training regularly in safety meetings to ensure the effectiveness of the CHP.

As part of the assessment of the training program, the safety manager will obtain input from employees regarding the training they have received, and their suggestions for improving it.

Index

SAFETY CERTIFIED™
The Safety and Risk Management People

SafetyCertified has two brand new web-sites for everything you need in OSHA training:

1. www.safetycertified.com

Our main web-site has been updated with a new look and easy navigation! What's new?

- Easy navigation
- More tools
- New products
- Simple ordering
- Online chat

- Informative content
- Helpful online demo
- Instant-access Desktop tool
- Updated graphics
- And more!

2. www.oshaanswerbook.com

This new web-site is dedicated specifically to our publications. It is an excellent resource for all of your safety training needs.